FRAMEWORK
FOR
FAMILIES

By

J. Paul Reno

Pastor and Author

Framework For Families

Copyrighted © by Pastor Paul Reno
Hagerstown, MD
March, 2015

ISBN 978-0-9860808-6-9

Published by
Blessed Hope Publishers
Hagerstown, MD

Publishing and Formatting Assisted by
The Old Paths Publications
142 Gold Flume Way
Cleveland, GA 30528
Web address: www.theoldpathspublications.com
Email address: TOP@theoldpathspublications.com

All Scripture quotations in this book are taken from the *King James Version* of the Bible.

"All scripture is given by inspiration of God, and is profitable for doctrine, for reproof, for correction, for instruction in righteousness.

That the man of God may be perfect, thoroughly furnished unto all good works."

(II Tim. 3:16, 17)

DEDICATION

To my wife, Carolyn, my faithful partner in marriage, prayer and ministry, for her love, encouragement, wisdom, assistance and over 50 years of precious memories:

To my five children for their love, honor, prayers and service to Christ and His Kingdom:

To The Bible Brethren Church for their support and desire to obey the Bible.

Paul Reno
March, 2015

FOREWORD

Early in our marriage and ministry, Dr. Don Moffat told us of his father-in-law, Dr. Robert Ketchum, who had prayed that one of John Reno's (my father) five sons would be called to the ministry. At about the same time we heard about Dr. L. E. Maxwell's family and learned that all of his children were saved and actively serving the Lord.

We began an intensive study of the Scriptures to see if we could find the means by which God might so bless our family. In the process, we found answers to many of the questions and problems of the people to whom we ministered. The Bible does have the answers!

The notes to follow were developed over 45+ years of teaching and preaching. They have proved profitable in several countries and cultures. May God bless them to your prayerful use and may they result in the establishing of Biblical homes.

Pastor Paul Reno
Hagerstown, MD
March, 2015

TABLE OF CONTENTS

DEDICATION 3
FOREWORD 4
TABLE OF CONTENTS 5
CHAPTER I: INTRODUCTION TO THE FAMILY 9
    A. Instituted by God 9
    B. High Priority 10
    C. Purposes 10
CHAPTER II: HUSBAND-WIFE RELATIONSHIP 11
    Eph. 5:17 11
    Eph. 5:22-33 11
    I Pet. 3:1-7 14
    I Tim. 3:2-13 16
    I Tim. 5:8 17
    Titus 2:1-8 17
    Tit. 2:1 17
    I Cor. 7:1-40 18
CHAPTER III: PARENT-CHILD RELATIONSHIP 25
    A. Results that are possible 25
        II Tim. 1:5 25
        II Tim. 3:15 25
        Gen. 37:2 25
        I Sam. 3:1-4 26
        I Sam. 17:33 26
        Jer. 1:7 26
        Daniel 1:3, 4, 8 27
        Luke 2:41-47, 52 27
    B. God's Means of Training Children 28
        Deut. 6:4-12 28
        Psalm. 78:1-8 29
        Prov. 22:6 30
        Ezek. 16:44 31
        Eph. 6:1-4 32
        Matt. 15:22-28 33
        Mark 9:17-24 33

TABLE OF CONTENTS

  Mark 10:13-16 34
 C. Discipline 35
  Prov. 22:6 35
  Prov. 13:24 36
  Prov. 19:18 36
  Prov. 20:30 37
  Prov. 22:15 37
  Prov. 23: 13, 14 37
  Prov. 29:15-17 38
CHAPTER IV: HUSBAND PREPARATION 39
 A. The Necessity of Preparation 39
  I Pet. 3:7 39
 B. Areas of Knowledge 40
  I Pet. 3:7 40
  I John 2:12-14 43
  I Tim. 5:8 43
 C. Obtaining Preparation 44
CHAPTER V: WIFE PREPARATION 47
 A. The Necessity of Preparation 47
  I Pet. 2:25-3:9 47
  Prov. 31:10-31 48
 B. Means of Preparation 51
CHAPTER VI: SINGLE PARENT FAMILY 55
 A. Such is not planned nor best in the eyes of God. 55
 B. These do occur due to tragedies: 55
 C. Heavy load on single parent, - handicap on the child or children. 55
 D. Christians are expected to assist the fatherless and widows .. 56
  James 1:27 56
CHAPTER VII: FAMILY IDENTITY 61
 A. Origin of Identity 61
 B. Heritage and History 61
 C. Reputation and Character 62
 D. Goals, Standards, and Values 62
 E. Manners 63
 F. Relationships with Relatives 64
 G. Nature and Attitude Towards Jobs 64

H. Balance with Church and Government.................................65
CHAPTER VIII: SPIRITUAL FUNCTIONS OF THE FAMILY.....................67
A. The Home..67
B. Training Children Spiritually..67
C. The Family Spiritual Life..69
CHAPTER IX: EDUCATIONAL FOUNDATIONS.................................75
A. Education..75
B. Learning..76
C. Reading...82
D. Time Usage...83
CHAPTER X: FINANCIAL OPERATIONS......................................85
A. Importance...85
B. Poverty – Its Causes and Cures.....................................85
C. Working...90
D. Business..93
E. Borrowing, Co-signing, Lending, Interest.........................93
F. Priorities...100
G. Savings and Investments...101
H. Estates, Wills, Inheritances.......................................103
I. Giving...106
J. Covetousness or Contentment..106
CHAPTER XI: RECREATIONAL POSSIBILITIES............................111
A. Family Time...111
B. Vacations..111
C. Sports...111
D. Bible Conferences, Camping, Camp Meetings.....................112
E. Considerations...112
CHAPTER XII: RESTRAINING ADULT CHILDREN FROM SIN................113
A. Responsibility...113
   I Sam. 3:13..113
   I Sam. 2:12-17, 22...113
   I Sam. 2:25; 3:13, 14...114
   I Sam. 3:13..114
B. Opportunity...116
   I Sam. 3:13..116
C. Methods or Tools..118
   Prov. 22:6...118

TABLE OF CONTENTS

Acts 3:12 118
Matt: 7:7, 8 119
Gen. 26:34, 35; 28: 6-9 119
I Sam. 3:12-14 120
James 1:6-8 121
II Tim. 2:24-26 121
Luke 15:11-32 122
Gal. 5:7, 8 123
I Sam. 2:23-25 123
II Tim. 2:24-26 124
Heb. 11:24-26 124
ABOUT THE AUTHOR..**125**

CHAPTER I

INTRODUCTION TO THE FAMILY

A. Instituted by God

1. Created and started by God (**Gen. 2:23, 24; 3:16-19**).

Gen. 2:23: And Adam said, This is now bone of my bones, and flesh of my flesh: she shall be called Woman, because she was taken out of Man. **(Genesis 2:23),** *24 Therefore shall a man leave his father and his mother, and shall cleave unto his wife: and they shall be one flesh.* **(Genesis 2:24),** *16 Unto the woman he said, I will greatly multiply thy sorrow and thy conception; in sorrow thou shalt bring forth children; and thy desire shall be to thy husband, and he shall rule over thee. 17 And unto Adam he said, Because thou hast hearkened unto the voice of thy wife, and hast eaten of the tree, of which I commanded thee, saying, Thou shalt not eat of it: cursed is the ground for thy sake; in sorrow shalt thou eat of it all the days of thy life; 18 Thorns also and thistles shall it bring forth to thee; and thou shalt eat the herb of the field; 19 In the sweat of thy face shalt thou eat bread, till thou return unto the ground; for out of it wast thou taken: for dust thou art, and unto dust shalt thou return.* (**Genesis 3:16-19**)

- ➢ Therefore the rules are God's rules.
- ➢ Man has no right to tamper with the institution or its rules.

2. Established with details before the details were needed.
3. First of the three God-originated institutions.
    - ➢ Others are Government and Church.
    - ➢ Never conflicts or competes with the Government or Church by God's definitions.

CHAPTER 1: INTRODUCTION TO THE FAMILY

> ➢ Church and Government should not infringe on the family.

B. High Priority

1. First institution created.
2. More Scriptures given to details of correct operation than other two institutions.
3. Serves as the basis of right Government and true Churches.
4. Clear picture of salvation.
5. Area Satan attacks (**I Tim. 4:1-3:** *1 Now the Spirit speaketh expressly, that in the latter times some shall depart from the faith, giving heed to seducing spirits, and doctrines of devils; 2 Speaking lies in hypocrisy; having their conscience seared with a hot iron; 3 Forbidding to marry, and commanding to abstain from meats, which God hath created to be received with thanksgiving of them which believe and know the truth.* **1 Timothy 4:1-3**).

C. Purposes

1. God's way of perpetuating the human race.
2. Foundation of local Churches, good Government and real civilization.
3. Basis for education, the economy, peace, and obedience to the law.
4. Produce laborers for God, Church, Country, and the good of mankind.
5. Self-perpetuating.

CHAPTER II

HUSBAND-WIFE RELATIONSHIP

Eph. 5:17

Eph. 5:17: *Wherefore be ye not unwise, but understanding what the will of the Lord is.* **(Ephesians 5:17)**

1. We should both know and understand what the will of the Lord is.
2. This applies to the family.

Eph. 5:22-33

vs. Eph. 5:22: *Wives, submit yourselves unto your own husbands, as unto the Lord.*
1. Wives are to submit to husbands.
2. Husbands are to give the wives something to submit to.

vs. Eph. 5:23: *For the husband is the head of the wife, even as Christ is the head of the church: and he is the saviour of the body.*
3. Principle of headship applies to both church and wife.
   - ➢ **Num. 30:1-15** – O.T. Headship

Num. 30:1: *And Moses spake unto the heads of the tribes concerning the children of Israel, saying, This is the thing which the LORD hath commanded. **2** If a man vow a vow unto the LORD, or swear an oath to bind his soul with a bond; he shall not break his word, he shall do according to all that proceedeth out of his mouth. **3** If a woman also vow a vow unto the LORD, and bind herself by a bond, being in her father's house in her youth; **4** And her father hear her vow, and her bond wherewith she hath bound her soul, and her father shall hold his peace at her: then all her vows shall stand, and every bond wherewith she hath bound her soul shall stand. **5** But if her father disallow her in the* *day that he heareth; not any of her vows, or of her bonds wherewith she hath bound her soul, shall stand: and the LORD shall forgive her, because her father disallowed her.* **6** *And if she had at all an husband, when she vowed, or uttered ought out of her lips, wherewith she bound her soul;* **7** *And her husband heard it, and held his peace at her in the day that he heard it: then her vows shall stand, and her bonds wherewith she bound her soul shall stand.* **8** *But if her husband disallowed her on the day that he heard it; then he shall make her vow which she vowed, and that which she uttered with her lips, wherewith she bound her soul, of none effect: and the LORD shall forgive her.* **9** *But every vow of a widow, and of her that is divorced, wherewith they have bound their souls, shall stand against her.* **10** *And if she vowed in her husband's house, or bound her soul by a bond with an oath;* **11** *And her husband heard it, and held his peace at her, and disallowed her not: then all her vows shall stand, and every bond wherewith she bound her soul shall stand.* **12** *But if her husband hath utterly made them void on the day he heard them; then whatsoever proceeded out of her lips concerning her vows, or concerning the bond of her soul, shall not stand: her husband hath made them void; and the LORD shall forgive her.* **13** *Every vow, and every binding oath to afflict the soul, her husband may establish it, or her husband may make it void.* **14** *But if her husband altogether hold his peace at her from day to day; then he establisheth all her vows, or all her bonds, which are upon her: he confirmeth them, because he held his peace at her in the day that he heard them.* **15** *But if he shall any ways make them void after that he hath heard them; then he shall bear her iniquity.* **Numbers 30:1-15**

> ➢ **I. Cor. 11:3** – New Testament Headship

But I would have you know, that the head of every man is Christ; and the head of the woman is the man; and the head of Christ is God. (**1 Corinthians 11:3)**

> ➢ **I Tim. 2:12-14** – Reason for Headship

12 If we suffer, we shall also reign with him: if we deny him, he also will deny us: 13 If we believe not, yet he abideth faithful: he cannot deny himself. 14 Of these things put them in remembrance, charging them before the Lord that they strive not about words to no profit, but to the subverting of the hearers. **2 Timothy 2:12-14**

Headship is an umbrella principle of protection.

vs. Eph. 5:24: *Therefore as the church is subject unto Christ, so let the wives be to their own husbands in every thing.*

4. Extent of subjection is "in everything."
5. Authority also carries responsibility.
6. Importance of a right Church for a right marriage.

vs. Eph. 5:25: *Husbands, love your wives, even as Christ also loved the church, and gave himself for it.*

7. Husband is to love the wife with example and extent given.
8. Three types of love:
    - sensual – flesh
    - getting – self
    - giving – heart
9. Wife should give something to love.

vss. Eph. 5:26, 27: *That he might sanctify and cleanse it with the washing of water by the word, 27 That he might present it to himself a glorious church, not having spot, or wrinkle, or any such thing; but that it should be holy and without blemish.*

10. Right loving can produce positive changes in wife.

vs. Eph. 5:28: *So ought men to love their wives as their own bodies. He that loveth his wife loveth himself.*

11. Women respond to love, men to subjection.

vs. Eph. 5:31: *For this cause shall a man leave his father and mother, and shall be joined unto his wife, and they two shall be one flesh.*

12. Man is to leave home to become married.
13. Two become one, - no longer two.

vs. Eph. 5:33: *Nevertheless let every one of you in particular so love his wife even as himself; and the wife see that she reverence her husband.*

14. Wife to reverence her husband.
15. Submission is active, not passive. Wrong is to be protested and responsibility is moved only when obedience is required.
16. Husband is to give commands in perfection as Jesus does. ... (This is not a club for a wife to use against her husband).

I Pet. 3:1-7

vs. 1 Pet. 3:1: *Likewise, ye wives, be in subjection to your own husbands; that, if any obey not the word, they also may without the word be won by the conversation of the wives;*

1. Wife's submission can bring husband's correction of life and/or conversion.
   - ➤ Thus, marital problems can be solved by God's power through either the husband or the wife. It only takes one if the other does not leave.

vs. 1 Pet. 3:2: *While they behold your chaste conversation coupled with fear.*

2. Husband responds to chaste (proper and pure) life coupled with fear (humble, respectful, fear of God more than man).

vss. 1 Pet. 3:3-5: *Whose adorning let it not be that outward adorning of plaiting the hair, and of wearing of gold, or of putting on of apparel; 4 But let it be the hidden man of the heart, in that which is not corruptible, even the ornament of a meek and quiet spirit, which is in the sight of God of great price. 5 For after this manner in the old time* *the holy women also, who trusted in God, adorned themselves, being in subjection unto their own husbands:*

3. Appeal of wife to husband is to be through the life (inner) rather than the physical and appearance (outer).
4. It is not trust in husband but in God to honor His Word when the wife is in subjection.
5. The subjection is to be exclusively to her own husband. Problems arise on jobs when she works for a man.

vs. 1 Pet. 3:6: *Even as Sara obeyed Abraham, calling him lord: whose daughters ye are, as long as ye do well, and are not afraid with any amazement.*

6. LORD – Lord Concept ... Headship Principle.
7. Marriage and salvation picture (**Isa. 33:22**). *For the LORD is our judge, the LORD is our lawgiver, the LORD is our king; he will save us.* **Isaiah 33:22**
8. Sarah obeyed Abraham but trusted in God. She did not doubt nor fear.

vs. 1 Pet. 3:7: *Likewise, ye husbands, dwell with them according to knowledge, giving honour unto the wife, as unto the weaker vessel, and as being heirs together of the grace of life; that your prayers be not hindered.*

9. Likewise, husbands are to both have and exercise knowledge for their position.
10. Prayer life of both is affected by right relationship. (**Matt. 18:18-20: 18** *Verily I say unto you, Whatsoever ye shall bind on earth shall be bound in heaven: and whatsoever ye shall loose on earth shall be loosed in heaven.* **19** *Again I say unto you, That if two of you shall agree on earth as touching any thing that they shall ask, it shall be done for them of my Father which is in heaven.* **20** *For where two or three are gathered together in my name, there am I in the midst of them.* **Matthew 18:18-20**).

CHAPTER 2: HUSBAND-WIFE RELATIONSHIP

I Tim. 3:2-13

2 A bishop then must be blameless, the husband of one wife, vigilant, sober, of good behaviour, given to hospitality, apt to teach; 3 Not given to wine, no striker, not greedy of filthy lucre; but patient, not a brawler, not covetous; 4 One that ruleth well his own house, having his children in subjection with all gravity; 5 (For if a man know not how to rule his own house, how shall he take care of the church of God?) 6 Not a novice, lest being lifted up with pride he fall into the condemnation of the devil. 7 Moreover he must have a good report of them which are without; lest he fall into reproach and the snare of the devil. 8 Likewise must the deacons be grave, not doubletongued, not given to much wine, not greedy of filthy lucre; 9 Holding the mystery of the faith in a pure conscience. 10 And let these also first be proved; then let them use the office of a deacon, being found blameless. 11 Even so must their wives be grave, not slanderers, sober, faithful in all things. 12 Let the deacons be the husbands of one wife, ruling their children and their own houses well. 13 For they that have used the office of a deacon well purchase to themselves a good degree, and great boldness in the faith which is in Christ Jesus. **1 Timothy 3:2-13**

1. Deacons and Pastors are to live such lives that the Church, new converts, and the world have a clear illustration and pattern of the Christian Home.

vss. 1 Tim. 3:4, 5: *One that ruleth well his own house, having his children in subjection with all gravity; 5 (For if a man know not how to rule his own house, how shall he take care of the church of God?)*

2. Husband is to rule the house.
3. Husband is to have the children in subjection.

vs. 1 Tim 3:11: *Even so must their wives be grave, not slanderers, sober, faithful in all things.*

4. Wife is to be grave, not a slanderer, sober, and faithful in all things.

I Tim. 5:8

But if any provide not for his own, and specially for those of his own house, he hath denied the faith, and is worse than an infidel. **1 Timothy 5:8**

1. Husband to provide.

vss. 1 Tim 3:14, 15: *I will therefore that the younger women marry, bear children, guide the house, give none occasion to the adversary to speak reproachfully. 15 For some are already turned aside after Satan.* **1 Timothy 5:14-15**

2. Women are to marry, bear children, guide the house, live above reproach, and care for relatives.

Titus 2:1-8

vs. Tit. 2:1: *But speak thou the things which become sound doctrine:*

vs. Tit. 2:2: *That the aged men be sober, grave, temperate, sound in faith, in charity, in patience.*

1. Older men have responsibilities as examples.

vs. Tit. 2:3: *The aged women likewise, that they be in behaviour as becometh holiness, not false accusers, not given to much wine, teachers of good things;*

2. Older women are responsible to be both an example and to teach younger women.

vss. 2:4, 5: *That they may teach the young women to be sober, to love their husbands, to love their children, 5 To be discreet, chaste, keepers at home, good, obedient to their own husbands, that the word of God be not blasphemed.*

CHAPTER 2: HUSBAND-WIFE RELATIONSHIP

3. Younger women to be taught as to life, relationship to husband, love of children, and keepers at home. Right living in these areas keeps God's Word from being blasphemed.

vss. Tit. 2:6-8: *Young men likewise exhort to be sober minded. **7** In all things shewing thyself a pattern of good works: in doctrine shewing uncorruptness, gravity, sincerity, **8** Sound speech, that cannot be condemned; that he that is of the contrary part may be ashamed, having no evil thing to say of you.*

4. Younger men to be taught regarding living as an example and an embarrassment to the devil.

I Cor. 7:1-40

vss.1 Cor. 7:1, 2, 9: *Now concerning the things whereof ye wrote unto me: It is good for a man not to touch a woman.* **1 Corinthians 7:1** *Nevertheless, to avoid fornication, let every man have his own wife, and let every woman have her own husband.* **1 Corinthians 7:2** *But if they cannot contain, let them marry: for it is better to marry than to burn.* **1 Corinthians 7:9**

1. Right relationships protect the partner from sin.

vss. 1 Cor. 7:4, 5: 4 *The wife hath not power of her own body, but the husband: and likewise also the husband hath not power of his own body, but the wife. **5** Defraud ye not one the other, except it be with consent for a time, that ye may give yourselves to fasting and prayer; and come together again, that Satan tempt you not for your incontinency.* **1 Corinthians 7:4-5**

2. Not to withhold from each other except for fasting and prayer. No other exceptions.

vss. 1 Cor. 7:10, 11: 10 *And unto the married I command, yet not I, but the Lord, Let not the wife depart from her husband: **11** But and if* *she depart, let her remain unmarried, or be reconciled to her husband: and let not the husband put away his wife.* **1 Corinthians 7:10-11**

3. Commands of Jesus from the Gospels summarized.
    - **Matt. 5:31, 32** (Sermon on the Mount. *31 It hath been said, Whosoever shall put away his wife, let him give her a writing of divorcement: 32 But I say unto you, That whosoever shall put away his wife, saving for the cause of fornication, causeth her to commit adultery: and whosoever shall marry her that is divorced committeth adultery.* **Matthew 5:31-32**)
    - **Matt. 19:3-9** (Sermon beyond Jordan *3 The Pharisees also came unto him, tempting him, and saying unto him, Is it lawful for a man to put away his wife for every cause? 4 And he answered and said unto them, Have ye not read, that he which made them at the beginning made them male and female, 5 And said, For this cause shall a man leave father and mother, and shall cleave to his wife: and they twain shall be one flesh? 6 Wherefore they are no more twain, but one flesh. What therefore God hath joined together, let not man put asunder. 7 They say unto him, Why did Moses then command to give a writing of divorcement, and to put her away? 8 He saith unto them, Moses because of the hardness of your hearts suffered you to put away your wives: but from the beginning it was not so. 9 And I say unto you, Whosoever shall put away his wife, except it be for fornication, and shall marry another, committeth adultery: and whoso marrieth her which is put away doth commit adultery.* **Matthew 19:3-9**)
    - **Mark 10:1-12** (Sermon beyond Jordan *1 And he arose from thence, and cometh into the coasts of Judaea by the farther side of Jordan: and the people resort unto him again; and, as he was wont, he taught them again. 2 And*

*the Pharisees came to him, and asked him, Is it lawful for a man to put away his wife? tempting him. **3** And he answered and said unto them, What did Moses command you? **4** And they said, Moses suffered to write a bill of divorcement, and to put her away. **5** And Jesus answered and said unto them, For the hardness of your heart he wrote you this precept. **6** But from the beginning of the creation God made them male and female. **7** For this cause shall a man leave his father and mother, and cleave to his wife; **8** And they twain shall be one flesh: so then they are no more twain, but one flesh. **9** What therefore God hath joined together, let not man put asunder. **10** And in the house his disciples asked him again of the same matter. **11** And he saith unto them, Whosoever shall put away his wife, and marry another, committeth adultery against her. **12** And if a woman shall put away her husband, and be married to another, she committeth adultery.* **Mark 10:1-12)**

- **Luke 16:18** (Sermon on Repentance *Whosoever putteth away his wife, and marrieth another, committeth adultery: and whosoever marrieth her that is put away from her husband committeth adultery.* **Luke 16:18)**

vs. 1 Tim. 3:12: *Let the deacons be the husbands of one wife, ruling their children and their own houses well.*

4. Holy Spirit inspires commands through Paul.
    - Additional details.
    - No contradictions.

vs. 1 Cor 7:13: *And the woman which hath an husband that believeth not, and if he be pleased to dwell with her, let her not leave him.* **1 Corinthians 7:13**

5. Issue is of an unbelieving partner.

vs. 1 Cor 7:15: *But if the unbelieving depart, let him depart. A brother or a sister is not under bondage in such cases: but God hath called us to peace.* **1 Corinthians 7:15**

6. The bondage (bond) to make a marriage go is broken when the unbelieving departs. This in **no** way frees one from marriage to marry another (**John 4; Rom. 7:1-3; I Cor. 7:39;** etc.). They are to remain unmarried (in practice) as Jesus taught, or be reconciled (**I Cor. 7:11** *But and if she depart, let her remain unmarried, or be reconciled to her husband: and let not the husband put away his wife.* **1 Corinthians 7:11**).

vs. 1 Cor. 7:16: *For what knowest thou, O wife, whether thou shalt save thy husband? or how knowest thou, O man, whether thou shalt save thy wife?* **1 Corinthians 7:16**

7. As long as they stay together, God can operate through the believer on the lost.
8. Marriage is until the death of one of the partners (**Rom. 7:1-3: 1** *Know ye not, brethren, (for I speak to them that know the law,) how that the law hath dominion over a man as long as he liveth?* **2** *For the woman which hath an husband is bound by the law to her husband so long as he liveth; but if the husband be dead, she is loosed from the law of her husband.* **3** *So then if, while her husband liveth, she be married to another man, she shall be called an adulteress: but if her husband be dead, she is free from that law; so that she is no adulteress, though she be married to another man.* **Romans 7:1-3**)
9. Divorce does not end marriage (**John 4:17-18 17** *The woman answered and said, I have no husband. Jesus said unto her, Thou hast well said, I have no husband:* **18** *For thou hast had five husbands; and he whom thou now hast is not thy husband: in that saidst thou truly.* **John 4:17-18 Jer. 3:8, 11**

CHAPTER 2: HUSBAND-WIFE RELATIONSHIP

And I saw, when for all the causes whereby backsliding Israel committed adultery I had put her away, and given her a bill of divorce; yet her treacherous sister Judah feared not, but went and played the harlot also. **Jeremiah 3:8** *And the LORD said unto me, The backsliding Israel hath justified herself more than treacherous Judah.* **Jeremiah 3:11**) but is the equivalent **in God's eyes** to a legal separation. To remarry while a former spouse lives is to commit adultery (see point 3); enter into polygamy (**John 4:18, see above**); break a solemn promise and covenant, and be called of God a fool (**Eccl. 5:1-5:** *1 Keep thy foot when thou goest to the house of God, and be more ready to hear, than to give the sacrifice of fools: for they consider not that they do evil. 2 Be not rash with thy mouth, and let not thine heart be hasty to utter any thing before God: for God is in heaven, and thou upon earth: therefore let thy words be few. 3 For a dream cometh through the multitude of business; and a fool's voice is known by multitude of words. 4 When thou vowest a vow unto God, defer not to pay it; for he hath no pleasure in fools: pay that which thou hast vowed. 5 Better is it that thou shouldest not vow, than that thou shouldest vow and not pay.* **Ecclesiastes 5:1-5**); disqualify oneself from areas of future ministry (**Titus 1:6, I Tim. 3:2:** *6 If any be blameless, the husband of one wife, having faithful children not accused of riot or unruly.* **Titus 1:6: 2** *A bishop then must be blameless, the husband of one wife, vigilant, sober, of good behaviour, given to hospitality, apt to teach;* **1 Timothy 3:2**); deface the picture of salvation and security of the believer (**Eph. 5: look this up in your Bible**); and help undermine the foundation of civilized society.

10. There is forgiveness for those who so violate God's laws, – especially to those who did so ignorantly

(**Heb. 10:26, 27:** *26 For if we sin wilfully after that we have received the knowledge of the truth, there remaineth no more sacrifice for sins, 27 But a certain fearful looking for of judgment and fiery indignation, which shall devour the adversaries.* **Hebrews 10:26-27**) or who were wrongly taught. Forgiveness deals with the sin of remarriage, but cannot deal with the original marriage, as marriage itself is not sin.

11. This Biblical position of the sin of divorce and remarriage is so clear that John the Baptist was willing to die for it rather than soften his convictions. The later teachings of Jesus and Paul further clarify this and state it in far stronger terms than the Old Testament (John the Baptist's only Bible).

CHAPTER 2: HUSBAND-WIFE RELATIONSHIP

CHAPTER III

PARENT-CHILD RELATIONSHIP

A. Results that are possible

II Tim. 1:5

When I call to remembrance the unfeigned faith that is in thee, which dwelt first in thy grandmother Lois, and thy mother Eunice; and I am persuaded that in thee also. **2 Timothy 1:5**

1. Faith can be passed down from generation to generation.
2. This can be done even without the husband's cooperation.
3. A Timothy can be produced in the home.
4. Three questions need answering:
    a. Do I have it?
    b. How did I get it?
    c. Am I passing it on?

II Tim. 3:15

And that from a child thou hast known the holy scriptures, which are able to make thee wise unto salvation through faith which is in Christ Jesus. **2 Timothy 3:15**

1. Timothy **knew the Scriptures** from childhood on.
2. His mother did not wait until youth or his teen years.

Gen. 37:2

These are the generations of Jacob. Joseph, being seventeen years old, was feeding the flock with his brethren; and the lad was with the sons

CHAPTER 3: PARENT-CHILD RELATIONSHIP

of Bilhah, and with the sons of Zilpah, his father's wives: and Joseph brought unto his father their evil report. **Genesis 37:2**

1. Joseph had learned all he would ever be taught by the age of 17.
2. It was enough for him to be faithful and walk with God in difficult situations.

I Sam. 3:1-4

1 And the child Samuel ministered unto the LORD before Eli. And the word of the LORD was precious in those days; there was no open vision. 2 And it came to pass at that time, when Eli was laid down in his place, and his eyes began to wax dim, that he could not see; 3 And ere the lamp of God went out in the temple of the LORD, where the ark of God was, and Samuel was laid down to sleep; 4 That the LORD called Samuel: and he answered, Here am I. **1 Samuel 3:1-4**

1. Samuel was not a child.
2. God spoke to him rather than older people.

I Sam. 17:33

And Saul said to David, Thou art not able to go against this Philistine to fight with him: for thou art but a youth, and he a man of war from his youth. **1 Samuel 17:33**

1. David was a youth, but was ready and selected of God.
2. What kind of leaders are we producing among our youth compared to what God shows can be done?

Jer. 1:7

But the LORD said unto me, Say not, I am a child: for thou shalt go to all that I shall send thee, and whatsoever I command thee thou shalt speak. **Jeremiah 1:7**

1. Jeremiah was a child.
2. Some home produced a child that God called to preach.

Daniel 1:3, 4, 8

And the king spake unto Ashpenaz the master of his eunuchs, that he should bring certain of the children of Israel, and of the king's seed, and of the princes; **Daniel 1:3** *Children in whom was no blemish, but well favoured, and skilful in all wisdom, and cunning in knowledge, and understanding science, and such as had ability in them to stand in the king's palace, and whom they might teach the learning and the tongue of the Chaldeans.* **Daniel 1:4** *But Daniel purposed in his heart that he would not defile himself with the portion of the king's meat, nor with the wine which he drank: therefore he requested of the prince of the eunuchs that he might not defile himself.* **Daniel 1:8**

1. Daniel was a child.
2. His Godly training was finished in childhood, but was adequate to stand in a heathen religion and culture.

Luke 2:41-47, 52

41 Now his parents went to Jerusalem every year at the feast of the passover. 42 And when he was twelve years old, they went up to Jerusalem after the custom of the feast. 43 And when they had fulfilled the days, as they returned, the child Jesus tarried behind in Jerusalem; and Joseph and his mother knew not of it. 44 But they, supposing him to have been in the company, went a day's journey; and they sought him among their kinsfolk and acquaintance. 45 And when they found him not, they turned back again to Jerusalem, seeking him. 46 And it came to pass, that after three days they found him in the temple, sitting in the midst of the doctors, both hearing them, and asking them questions. 47 And all that heard him were astonished at his

CHAPTER 3: PARENT-CHILD RELATIONSHIP

understanding and answers. **Luke 2:41-47,** *And Jesus increased in wisdom and stature, and in favour with God and man.* **Luke 2:52**

1. Jesus was 12 years old.
2. He could ask and answer deep questions of theology at the temple.
3. His home training had Him prepared.
4. Over a period of 1700+ years, we have records of the successes possible (without Sunday School Christian schools, youth groups, Christian videos, Christian radio, etc). **God's methods still work** if we will only use them. They **cannot** be improved upon.

B. God's Means of Training Children
Deut. 6:4-12

4 Hear, O Israel: The LORD our God is one LORD: 5 And thou shalt love the LORD thy God with all thine heart, and with all thy soul, and with all thy might. 6 And these words, which I command thee this day, shall be in thine heart: 7 And thou shalt teach them diligently unto thy children, and shalt talk of them when thou sittest in thine house, and when thou walkest by the way, and when thou liest down, and when thou risest up. 8 And thou shalt bind them for a sign upon thine hand, and they shall be as frontlets between thine eyes. 9 And thou shalt write them upon the posts of thy house, and on thy gates. 10 And it shall be, when the LORD thy God shall have brought thee into the land which he sware unto thy fathers, to Abraham, to Isaac, and to Jacob, to give thee great and goodly cities, which thou buildedst not, 11 And houses full of all good things, which thou filledst not, and wells digged, which thou diggedst not, vineyards and olive trees, which thou plantedst not; when thou shalt have eaten and be full; 12 Then beware lest thou forget the

LORD, which brought thee forth out of the land of Egypt, from the house of bondage. **Deuteronomy 6:4-12**

1. The Word must first be in the heart (not head) of parent and then be taught to children. Don't traffic in unfelt or unlived truths. (**Ezra 7:10** *For Ezra had prepared his heart to seek the law of the LORD, and to do it, and to teach in Israel statutes and judgments.*; **Acts 1:1** *The former treatise have I made, O Theophilus, of all that Jesus began both to do and teach,*; **Matt. 23:3** *All therefore whatsoever they bid you observe, that observe and do; but do not ye after their works: for they say, and do not.*)

2. Almost all the book of Deut. was Moses' farewell address. Thus the "these words" applies to what was preached that day. Don't avoid the teaching of the Law to children. It is basic (**Psalm. 119: 126, 165** *I have declared my ways, and thou heardest me: teach me thy statutes.* **Psalms 119:26** *Great peace have they which love thy law: and nothing shall offend them.* **Psalms 119:165; Hosea 4:6** *My people are destroyed for lack of knowledge: because thou hast rejected knowledge, I will also reject thee, that thou shalt be no priest to me: seeing thou hast forgotten the law of thy God, I will also forget thy children.* **Hosea 4:6**).

3. Teaching must be thorough, continual, at all times of the day, not just at devotions. It should be natural and normal to our conversation.

Psalm. 78:1-8

1 Maschil of Asaph. Give ear, O my people, to my law: incline your ears to the words of my mouth. 2 I will open my mouth in a parable: I will utter dark sayings of old: 3 Which we have heard and known, and our fathers have told us. 4 We will not hide them from their children, shewing to the generation to come the praises of the LORD, and his strength, and his wonderful works that he hath done. 5 For he established a testimony in Jacob, and appointed a law in Israel, which he commanded our fathers, that they should make them known to their children: 6 That the generation to come might know them, even the children which should be born; who should arise and declare them to their children: 7 That they might set their hope in God, and not forget the works of God, but keep his commandments: 8 And might not be as their fathers, a stubborn and rebellious generation; a generation that set not their heart aright, and whose spirit was not stedfast with God. **Psalms 78:1-8**

1. Our teaching is to be thorough enough that our children will see the importance of teaching their children (**vs. 5**) well enough that another two generations will be taught (**vs. 6**) etc.
2. We must look to influence four generations and more if we can.
3. Failure brings God's judgment on future generations.

Prov. 22:6

Train up a child in the way he should go: and when he is old, he will not depart from it. **Proverbs 22:6**

1. Training will affect the path they follow all their life.
2. Success or failure in the training is evidenced by the product.
3. Proper training will be:
    a) against their will
    b) with tenderness, affection, and patience
    c) with understanding of our responsibility

d) with the emphasis on the good of their soul
e) to a thorough knowledge of the Bible
f) to a life of prayer
g) to a habit of diligence
h) to a desire to worship God privately and in a right church
i) to a spirit of faith
j) to a habit of obedience
k) to a habit of always speaking the truth
l) to a habit of right time usage
m) with a constant fear of **over** indulgence or spoiling them
n) to properly handle money
o) remembering continually how God trains His children
p) remembering your own past and struggles
q) remembering continually the influence of your own example
r) remembering continually the promises of Scripture

(Most of these are amplified upon by J. C. Ryle in *Duties of Parents*.)

Ezek. 16:44

Behold, every one that useth proverbs shall use this proverb against thee, saying, As is the mother, so is her daughter. **Ezekiel 16:44**

1. As is the mother, so is the daughter.
2. God designed the laws from creation that we reproduce after our kind. (**Gen. 1:11, 12, 21, 24, 25** *And God said, Let*

the earth bring forth grass, the herb yielding seed, and the fruit tree yielding fruit after his kind, whose seed is in itself, upon the earth: and it was so. **Genesis 1:11,** *And the earth brought forth grass, and herb yielding seed after his kind, and the tree yielding fruit, whose seed was in itself, after his kind: and God saw that it was good.* **Genesis 1:12,** *And God created great whales, and every living creature that moveth, which the waters brought forth abundantly, after their kind, and every winged fowl after his kind: and God saw that it was good.* **Genesis 1:21, 24** *And God said, Let the earth bring forth the living creature after his kind, cattle, and creeping thing, and beast of the earth after his kind: and it was so. 25 And God made the beast of the earth after his kind, and cattle after their kind, and every thing that creepeth upon the earth after his kind: and God saw that it was good.* **Genesis 1:24-25**). Thus we should be able to understand and deal with our children far better than with anyone else's.

3. What we are, our children are likely to become.

Eph. 6:1-4

1 Children, obey your parents in the Lord: for this is right. 2 Honour thy father and mother; (which is the first commandment with promise;) 3 That it may be well with thee, and thou mayest live long on the earth. 4 And, ye fathers, provoke not your children to wrath: but bring them up in the nurture and admonition of the Lord. **Ephesians 6:1-4**

1. Fathers are held accountable by God for the proper raising of children.
2. Children are to respect, honor, and obey their parents (5th commandment).
3. Fathers, in particular, should take care not to provoke their children to anger.

4. Nurture has to do with feeding and caring for needs (the staff).
5. Admonishing has to do with warning and correction (the rod).

Matt. 15:22-28

22 And, behold, a woman of Canaan came out of the same coasts, and cried unto him, saying, Have mercy on me, O Lord, thou Son of David; my daughter is grievously vexed with a devil. 23 But he answered her not a word. And his disciples came and besought him, saying, Send her away; for she crieth after us. 24 But he answered and said, I am not sent but unto the lost sheep of the house of Israel. 25 Then came she and worshipped him, saying, Lord, help me. 26 But he answered and said, It is not meet to take the children's bread, and to cast it to dogs. 27 And she said, Truth, Lord: yet the dogs eat of the crumbs which fall from their masters' table. 28 Then Jesus answered and said unto her, O woman, great is thy faith: be it unto thee even as thou wilt. And her daughter was made whole from that very hour. **Matthew 15:22-28**

1. A desperate mother brought her daughter to Jesus.
2. Jesus can deal with demon-controlled children.

Mark 9:17-24

17 And one of the multitude answered and said, Master, I have brought unto thee my son, which hath a dumb spirit; 18 And wheresoever he taketh him, he teareth him: and he foameth, and gnasheth with his teeth, and pineth away: and I spake to thy disciples that they should cast him out; and they could not. 19 He answereth him, and saith, O faithless generation, how long shall I be with you? how long shall I suffer you? bring him unto me. 20 And they brought him unto him: and when he saw him, straightway the spirit tare him; and he fell on the ground, and wallowed foaming. 21 And he asked his father, How long is it ago since this came unto him? And he said, Of a child. **22** *And ofttimes it hath cast him into the fire, and into the waters, to destroy him: but if thou canst do any thing, have compassion on us, and help us.* **23** *Jesus said unto him, If thou canst believe, all things are possible to him that believeth.* **24** *And straightway the father of the child cried out, and said with tears, Lord, I believe; help thou mine unbelief.* **Mark 9:17-24**

1. A frustrated father brings his boy to Jesus.
2. Disciples had failed; the boy is young, but the case must not wait.
3. Parents must know how to commit their troubled children to Jesus for deliverance.

Mark 10:13-16

13 And they brought young children to him, that he should touch them: and his disciples rebuked those that brought them. **14** *But when Jesus saw it, he was much displeased, and said unto them, Suffer the little children to come unto me, and forbid them not: for of such is the kingdom of God.* **15** *Verily I say unto you, Whosoever shall not receive the kingdom of God as a little child, he shall not enter therein.* **16** *And he took them up in his arms, put his hands upon them, and blessed them.* **Mark 10:13-16**

1. Little children should be brought to Jesus for blessing.
2. We are so Biblically ignorant today that we know little about blessing others, much less getting Jesus to bless children.
3. Consider that right training prepares a child to receive the blessing.

C. Discipline
Prov. 22:6

Train up a child in the way he should go: and when he is old, he will not depart from it. **Proverbs 22:6**

1. **"Train"** implies effort and an organized plan.
2. **"Up"** gives direction. Our sinful nature normally heads downward (**Prov. 29:15b:** *The rod and reproof give wisdom: but a child left to himself bringeth his mother to shame.* **Proverbs 29:15**). Training up a child who naturally heads downward creates tension and differences (**Eph. 6:4:** *And, ye fathers, provoke not your children to wrath: but bring them up in the nurture and admonition of the Lord.* **Ephesians 6:4**).
3. **"A child"** is when we must start. The first five years are essential. To start at 6-10 years of age is difficult, 11-14 years old is nearly too late, and 15 years old and up will require a miracle of God's intervention.
4. **"In the way"** is where most parents miss it. This requires:
    a. knowing where you are headed with your child,
    b. knowing the particular path God wants for each individual child ("he", not "they"),
    c. getting the child into his own particular way,
    d. keeping the child in his own particular path,
    e. being in the right way for yourself, and
    f. knowing the schedule of training and methods to reach the goal.
5. **"Not depart from it"** shows that the way was so established that the child never left it. This is **not** a promise that they will come back to it.

CHAPTER 3: PARENT-CHILD RELATIONSHIP

6. Parents need to know each of their children, their differences, their individual needs, and their different goals. This needs to be known at an early age and is not the choice of the parents, as the child is only on loan from God (**Psm. 127:3:** *Lo, children are an heritage of the LORD: and the fruit of the womb is his reward.* **Psalms 127:3**).
7. Discipline is a part of the training and must be applied to help the child stay (or get back on) course. All discipline is to be goal-related and never a release of frustrations.

Prov. 13:24

He that spareth his rod hateth his son: but he that loveth him chasteneth him betimes. **Proverbs 13:24**

1. Sparing the rod (limiting, avoiding, or refusing to use) is a result of hating a child. True love will discipline **in God's way**.
2. **"Spare"** indicates that every child will have a need.
3. **"Betimes"** indicates we need to know the right times.
4. Love is evidenced by use of a rod to chasten.
5. The instrument God commands to be used is a rod, not a paddle, belt, whip, switch, or hand (the symbol of love).
6. A rod is a symbol, Biblically, of authority and judgment. It is effective as it works on little children as well as big teen boys (even by weakened mothers). It is severe and thus serves the parent to **not** just swing away. It is larger than a switch and smaller than a club.

Prov. 19:18

Chasten thy son while there is hope, and let not thy soul spare for his crying. **Proverbs 19:18**

1. Chastening is to try to reach for goals.
2. Their crying is not to make you let up on correction.
3. Think on other children who have gone wrong and now yours might if you forget your goals (hope).

Prov. 20:30

The blueness of a wound cleanseth away evil: so do stripes the inward parts of the belly. **Proverbs 20:30**

1. A thorough job results in evil being cleansed away.
2. Within reason and governed by love, God promises that you can "beat it out of your child." It happened to me.
3. The ugly, sickening, painful, unsightly is needed for healing.
4. This is **not** a license to whale away on a child.

Prov. 22:15

Foolishness is bound in the heart of a child; but the rod of correction shall drive it far from him. **Proverbs 22:15**

1. The rod drives natural foolishness out of a child's heart.
2. The rod is to correct behavior, not just punish it.

Prov. 23: 13, 14

13 *Withhold not correction from the child: for if thou beatest him with the rod, he shall not die.* **14** *Thou shalt beat him with the rod, and shalt deliver his soul from hell.* **Proverbs 23:13-14**

1. The rod of correction prolongs the life of a child. It will hinder teenage suicide, wild driving, etc.
2. The rod is an evidence of our love to them.
3. The rod, properly used, affects their being saved!

CHAPTER 3: PARENT-CHILD RELATIONSHIP

4. The rod teaches of the nature of God; prompt and proper judgment to come; and makes hell real.
5. There is a need for consistency and picturing of the nature of God.

Prov. 29:15-17

15 The rod and reproof give wisdom: but a child left to himself bringeth his mother to shame. 16 When the wicked are multiplied, transgression increaseth: but the righteous shall see their fall. 17 Correct thy son, and he shall give thee rest; yea, he shall give delight unto thy soul. **Proverbs 29:15-17**

1. The rod is to be used along with reproof.
2. Use or lack thereof results in wisdom or shame; increase or decrease in wickedness; and rest and delight for those obedient.

CHAPTER IV
HUSBAND PREPARATION

A. The Necessity of Preparation

I Pet. 3:7

Likewise, ye husbands, dwell with them according to knowledge, giving honour unto the wife, as unto the weaker vessel, and as being heirs together of the grace of life; that your prayers be not hindered. **1 Peter 3:7**

1. God expects husbands to dwell with their wives **"according to knowledge."**
2. One basis of marriage for husbands is **knowledge**, not ...

emotions	position	agreement
looks	pride	reputation
attraction	strength	ignorance
money	threats	learn-as-you-go
ability	intelligence	

3. Most men are unprepared for marriage and base the union on wrong foundations.
4. **Tests of knowledge** must be passed to get a license for:

Driving	Teaching	Welding	CPA
Architect	Lawyer	Minister	Nurse
First Aid	Plumber	Mechanic	CPR
Contractor	Engineer	Doctor	Banker
Electrician	Dentist	Ham Radio Operator	
Stock Broker	Chiropractor	Insurance Sales	

5. No test of knowledge for marriage and parenting!

CHAPTER 4: HUSBAND PREPARATION

6. **Knowledge** is one of the three bases for dwelling together properly. Also included are **"giving honor"** and **"heirs together."** Men must learn to honor their wife through love. They also should be honest spiritually and living as a godly saved man. Both of these require preparation before marriage.
7. A couple's prayer life is affected by the husband's preparation and function in these three areas.
8. Unprepared and/or dysfunctional husbands produce home problems and unanswered prayer.

B. Areas of Knowledge

I Pet. 3:7 (see the verse immediately above)

1. Areas of **knowledge** for use as well as teaching the next generation:
    - Salvation
    - Holy Living
    - Prayer
    - Witnessing
    - Serving God
    - Faith
    - Bible Teaching
    - Bible Doctrine
    - Pleasing God
    - Morality
    - Modesty
    - Establishing Values
    - Emotional Changes and Responses
    - Money
    - Business

- Causes of Poverty
- Saving
- Learning
- Education
- Different Stages of Life
- Husband/Wife Relationships
- Wife's Needs
- Knowing wife's thoughts, desires, reactions, background, values, etc.
- Providing for a Family
- Being an Example to the Family
- Raising Children
- Teaching Children
- Correcting Children
- Preparing Children for Life
- Preparing Children for Marriage
- Meeting financial, educational, emotional, spiritual, and physical needs of family
- Adjusting to better or worse, richer or poorer, sickness or health
- Manners
- Dress Concepts
- Use of Time
- Setting Goals
- Setting Priorities

2. **Giving of honor**

To the wife	Good manners
As the weaker vessel	Building her up
	Defending her
Humbly	Covering weak points

CHAPTER 4: HUSBAND PREPARATION

<u>Pointing out her good points</u>
<u>Always Respectful</u>
Rewarding her
Doing special things
Understand how to present her before an on-looking world
<u>Put on a pedestal as a queen</u>

3. As **heirs together** of the grace of life
   - No unequal yokes (**II Cor. 6:14-18: 14** *Be ye not unequally yoked together with unbelievers: for what fellowship hath righteousness with unrighteousness? and what communion hath light with darkness?* **15** *And what concord hath Christ with Belial? or what part hath he that believeth with an infidel?* **16** *And what agreement hath the temple of God with idols? for ye are the temple of the living God; as God hath said, I will dwell in them, and walk in them; and I will be their God, and they shall be my people.* **17** *Wherefore come out from among them, and be ye separate, saith the Lord, and touch not the unclean thing; and I will receive you,* **18** *And will be a Father unto you, and ye shall be my sons and daughters, saith the Lord Almighty.* **2 Corinthians 6:14-18**)
   - Understanding and evidencing grace in their life
   - Being at least an equal if not the superior spiritually so that they can be the leader
   - Definite prayer life that can be shared with a wife
   - Devotional life to share with a wife for their spiritual progress
   - Active involvement in a Biblical church for obedience, spiritual stability, oversight, help, encouragement, teaching, fellowship, examples, etc.

I John 2:12-14

12 I write unto you, little children, because your sins are forgiven you for his name's sake. 13 I write unto you, fathers, because ye have known him that is from the beginning. I write unto you, young men, because ye have overcome the wicked one. I write unto you, little children, because ye have known the Father. 14 I have written unto you, fathers, because ye have known him that is from the beginning. I have written unto you, young men, because ye are strong, and the word of God abideth in you, and ye have overcome the wicked one. **1 John 2:12-14**

4. **Spiritual progress** that is observable and measurable
   - Fathers should be all (plus) that the children and young men are
   - Should know God intimately from beginning to present in nature, acts, principles, desires, etc.

I Tim. 5:8

But if any provide not for his own, and specially for those of his own house, he hath denied the faith, and is worse than an infidel. **1 Timothy 5:8**

5. **Financial ability** to provide
   - Not to provide is to deny the faith
   - Not to provide is to be worse than an infidel
   - Preparation to provide is for **own household** as well as assisting family relatives
   - Preparation to provide for widowed mother(s) as well as aunts (**vs. 4**)
   - Ability and experience to earn and provide should be shown

CHAPTER 4: HUSBAND PREPARATION

Thus, preparation should be Mental, Emotional, Spiritual and Financial.

C. Obtaining Preparation

1. So many areas and details of preparation require time and effort to accomplish.
2. We should always be getting more preparation – never have enough.
3. Young boys begun early on such preparation may be ready for marriage by manhood.
4. The **BIBLE** offers great help through:
   Reading   Memorizing
   Studying   Hearing it preached
   Meditating   Hearing it taught
5. The **FAMILY** is a nourishing unit to prepare boys; especially the parents and home, grandparents, uncles and aunts, brothers and sisters.
   Teaching   Experience
   Observation   Attempt to improve
6. **GODLY SAINTS** are valuable assets to struggling men. Pastors and deacons have high requirements so that they can best illustrate in life.
   Watch   Ask
   Fellowship with   Listen
7. **BIBLICAL CHURCHES** create a spiritual environment that is often more "family" than relatives of our first birth. They will set proper examples, preach and teach on needed areas, assist in preparation, help those who failed to prepare, pray men through their struggles and create an atmosphere of help and healing for those in need.

8. **PRAYER** is not only asking God but also hearing from God. He still answers, gives help, leads and directs, and encourages.

CHAPTER 4: HUSBAND PREPARATION

CHAPTER V

WIFE PREPARATION

A. The Necessity of Preparation

I Pet. 2:25-3:9

For ye were as sheep going astray; but are now returned unto the Shepherd and Bishop of your souls. **1 Peter 2:25** *1 Likewise, ye wives, be in subjection to your own husbands; that, if any obey not the word, they also may without the word be won by the conversation of the wives; 2 While they behold your chaste conversation coupled with fear. 3 Whose adorning let it not be that outward adorning of plaiting the hair, and of wearing of gold, or of putting on of apparel; 4 But let it be the hidden man of the heart, in that which is not corruptible, even the ornament of a meek and quiet spirit, which is in the sight of God of great price. 5 For after this manner in the old time the holy women also, who trusted in God, adorned themselves, being in subjection unto their own husbands: 6 Even as Sara obeyed Abraham, calling him lord: whose daughters ye are, as long as ye do well, and are not afraid with any amazement. 7 Likewise, ye husbands, dwell with them according to knowledge, giving honour unto the wife, as unto the weaker vessel, and as being heirs together of the grace of life; that your prayers be not hindered. 8 Finally, be ye all of one mind, having compassion one of another, love as brethren, be pitiful, be courteous: 9 Not rendering evil for evil, or railing for railing: but contrariwise blessing; knowing that ye are thereunto called, that ye should inherit a blessing.* **1 Peter 3:1-9**

1. Attitudes and responses must be developed for success in marriage.
   Examples:
   - ➢ Subjection to husband (**vss. 1, 5**)

CHAPTER 5: WIFE PREPARATION

- ➢ Inner appeal rather than exterior (**vss. 3, 4**)
- ➢ Trust in God (**vss. 1, 5, 6**)
- ➢ Courteous, compassionate, and not argumentative (**vss. 8, 9**)

2. A practical level of spiritual development should be achieved.
   Examples:
   - ➢ Prayer life (**vs. 7**)
   - ➢ Heir of the grace of life (**vss. 7, 9**)
   - ➢ Holy (**vs. 5**)
   - ➢ Knowledgeable of Bible women (**vss. 5, 6**)
   - ➢ As sheep (**2:25**)

Prov. 31:10-31

10 Who can find a virtuous woman? for her price is far above rubies. 11 The heart of her husband doth safely trust in her, so that he shall have no need of spoil. 12 She will do him good and not evil all the days of her life. 13 She seeketh wool, and flax, and worketh willingly with her hands. 14 She is like the merchants' ships; she bringeth her food from afar. 15 She riseth also while it is yet night, and giveth meat to her household, and a portion to her maidens. 16 She considereth a field, and buyeth it: with the fruit of her hands she planteth a vineyard. 17 She girdeth her loins with strength, and strengtheneth her arms. 18 She perceiveth that her merchandise is good: her candle goeth not out by night. 19 She layeth her hands to the spindle, and her hands hold the distaff. 20 She stretcheth out her hand to the poor; yea, she reacheth forth her hands to the needy. 21 She is not afraid of the snow for her household: for all her household are clothed with scarlet. 22 She maketh herself coverings of tapestry; her clothing is silk and purple. 23 Her husband is known in the gates, when he sitteth among the elders of the land. 24 She maketh fine linen, and selleth it; and delivereth girdles unto *the merchant. **25** Strength and honour are her clothing; and she shall rejoice in time to come. **26** She openeth her mouth with wisdom; and in her tongue is the law of kindness. **27** She looketh well to the ways of her household, and eateth not the bread of idleness. **28** Her children arise up, and call her blessed; her husband also, and he praiseth her. **29** Many daughters have done virtuously, but thou excellest them all. **30** Favour is deceitful, and beauty is vain: but a woman that feareth the LORD, she shall be praised. **31** Give her of the fruit of her hands; and let her own works praise her in the gates.* **Proverbs 31:10-31**

3. Practical virtues of homemaking should be known and able to be practiced:
   - Keepers at home (**Titus 2:5:** *To be discreet, chaste, keepers at home, good, obedient to their own husbands, that the word of God be not blasphemed.* **Titus 2:5**)
   - Guide the house (**I Tim. 5:14:** *I will therefore that the younger women marry, bear children, guide the house, give none occasion to the adversary to speak reproachfully.* **1 Timothy 5:14**)
   - A worker (**Prov. 31:13:** etc. *She seeketh wool, and flax, and worketh willingly with her hands.* **Proverbs 31:13**)
   - Good shopper (**vs. 14:** *She is like the merchants' ships; she bringeth her food from afar.* **Proverbs 31:14**)
   - Good cook (**vs. 15:** *She riseth also while it is yet night, and giveth meat to her household, and a portion to her maidens.* **Proverbs 31:15**)
   - Not lazy or over sleeper (**vss. 15: see verse above, 27** *She looketh well to the ways of her household, and eateth not the bread of idleness.* **Proverbs 31:27**)
   - Able to invest and develop assets (**vss. 16:** *She considereth a field, and buyeth it: with the fruit of her*

hands she planteth a vineyard. **Proverbs 31:16 24** *She maketh fine linen, and selleth it; and delivereth girdles unto the merchant.* **Proverbs 31:24**)

- Cares for health and strength (**vs. 17** *She girdeth her loins with strength, and strengtheneth her arms.* **Proverbs 31:17**)
- Knows quality (**vss. 18, 22:** *She perceiveth that her merchandise is good: her candle goeth not out by night.* **Proverbs 31:18,** *She maketh herself coverings of tapestry; her clothing is silk and purple.* **Proverbs 31:22**)
- Cares for the needy (**vs. 20** *She stretcheth out her hand to the poor; yea, she reacheth forth her hands to the needy.* **Proverbs 31:20**)
- Plans ahead (**vs. 21, 27:** *She is not afraid of the snow for her household: for all her household are clothed with scarlet.* **Proverbs 31:21** *She looketh well to the ways of her household, and eateth not the bread of idleness.* **Proverbs 31:27**)
- Encourages and helps husband to be honored (**vs. 23:** *Her husband is known in the gates, when he sitteth among the elders of the land.* **Proverbs 31:23**)
- Works hard now to rejoice later (**vs. 25:** *Strength and honour are her clothing; and she shall rejoice in time to come.* **Proverbs 31:25**)
- Wise, kind, and a speaker (**vs. 26:** *She openeth her mouth with wisdom; and in her tongue is the law of kindness.* **Proverbs 31:26**)
- Praised by children and husband (**vs. 28:** *Her children arise up, and call her blessed; her husband also, and he praiseth her.* **Proverbs 31:28**)

4. Such qualities do not occur naturally. The home is the preparation place to develop these areas. The church and school may assist, but the home can best do the job. Children are the most helpless and take longest to reach maturity of any young in all of God's creation. This allows the needed time to properly prepare for marriage and the training of the next general for marriage, etc. Anything that wastes this needed training time is the enemy of the family, the church, and civilization.

B. Means of Preparation

1. Much of what applies to preparing of husbands will also apply to preparing wives.
   Examples:
   - Areas of knowledge (pgs. 40ff)
   - Obtaining preparation (pgs.39-51)
2. No wife is ever fully prepared. Even after marriage, learning is to continue (**Titus 2: 4, 5:** *4 That they may teach the young women to be sober, to love their husbands, to love their children, 5 To be discreet, chaste, keepers at home, good, obedient to their own husbands, that the word of God be not blasphemed.* **Titus 2:4-5**).
3. It is sufficient shock to adjust from:
   - Single to married status.
   - Submission to older, wiser, and experienced father to young, learning husband.
   - To leave shelter of home to establish a new home unit.
4. Anything that can be done to have adjusted to work load, responsibilities, and skill usage before marriage will ease

CHAPTER 5: WIFE PREPARATION

the marriage shock (**Lam. 3:27** shows that it is good to put the load on them while young. *It is good for a man that he bear the yoke in his youth.* **Lamentations 3:27**). To shelter, pamper, or overly protect them before marriage is to handicap the marriage and their future.

5. Parents should decide which of these areas should be developed, - to what degree at what age – in progression to reach a successful goal. While the desire is to reach all of these plus many more, there must be an established way for each daughter to be trained up in. Some have used the following structure to evaluate, encourage, and develop their children. It is only a suggestion and you may have something far better.

Initial goal is to have a child ready spiritually, attitude-wise, and with skills to be able to properly and successfully live on their own by 18, with a buffer period until 21 if needed. This doesn't mean they must move out but that they are able to and be in a satisfactory condition.

<u>At the age of 10,</u> their birthday is special and supper is eaten out with the parents in honor of this age ("two numbers old"). After the meal, a heart-to-heart talk is had. Privileges and responsibilities are shown to be related. A filing card with a small box in the middle is drawn, with the number 10 inside it. A larger box is then drawn around this box with 1 in it. They then help evaluate their progress on work skills, control of attitudes, spiritual concerns, desires for the future, etc. It is then

explained that their progress in privileges will be tied to their progress in certain areas of their practical lives. Also discussed are new areas of opportunity for learning and development by age 13 (gradually phased in as they are ready). The goal of 18 is also mentioned.

At 13, the entering of teen years, a repeat supper event occurs. This time we evaluate age 10-13, and lay plans on progress towards 16. New freedoms are discussed at this time as well as new areas of learning and responsibility.

At 16 (possible dating age?), we repeat and see how we are progressing towards the goal of 18. Possible dating, rules, curfews, purpose of dating, pre-approval of dates, etc. often are major topics. Discussion of needed skills and attitudes to become fit for marriage may also be discussed. Perhaps an easing away from the goal of 18 is needed if the youth is a "late bloomer."

At 18, we repeat and **perhaps** grant them the freedom to leave to live on their own without hard feelings if, or when, they might desire. It is not necessary nor expected, but if they want "to try their wings"; it isn't a reflection of failure at home, but rather, of success.

At age 21, they usually want to meet one more time for parents to analyze how they are doing!

CHAPTER 5: WIFE PREPARATION

While this particular structure is not perfect, it does encourage co-operation, measurability, understanding, and progress, etc. It has helped in many homes.

6. Parents should work together on an agreed general plan, and co-operate on working out the details as time goes forward.

CHAPTER VI

SINGLE PARENT FAMILY

A. Such is not planned nor best in the eyes of God.

B. These do occur due to tragedies:

1. Immorality – children born out of wedlock (Jephthah – **Judges 11:1:** *Now Jephthah the Gileadite was a mighty man of valour, and he was the son of an harlot: and Gilead begat Jephthah.* **Judges 11:1**)
2. Death – usually of the father (**James 1:27:** *Pure religion and undefiled before God and the Father is this, To visit the fatherless and widows in their affliction, and to keep himself unspotted from the world.* **James 1:27**)
3. Divorce or separation – result of hard hearts at best (Ishmael).

C. Heavy load on single parent, - handicap on the child or children.

1. Parent must be both father and mother, - something beyond their created abilities and home training.
2. Parent must understand both sides of child's background, with memory and experience in only one side.
3. Parent must teach child both sides of marriage without a daily model for the child to observe in the home.
4. Child must learn both masculinity and femininity in balance with only one side to see.

5. Child lacks picture of salvation in the home as shown by husband/wife relationship.
6. Child lacks normal experience base towards preparing for their own possible marriage.
7. Child lacks half of God's planned team in their raising.
8. Child may conclude that marriage relationships are not essential to be maintained as they survived without one.

D. Christians are expected to assist the fatherless and widows.

James 1:27

Pure religion and undefiled before God and the Father is this, To visit the fatherless and widows in their affliction, and to keep himself unspotted from the world. **James 1:27**

1. They should visit and spend time with them.
2. They should be aware of their conditions and needs, - especially the needs unique to such a situation.
3. Biblical means should be used to meet these needs as they arise.
4. Practical help is to be given.
5. Scriptures for churches to consider include:
    - **Ex. 22:22:** *Ye shall not afflict any widow, or fatherless child.* **Exodus 22:22**
    - **Num. 30:9:** *Ye shall offer no strange incense thereon, nor burnt sacrifice, nor meat offering; neither shall ye pour drink offering thereon.* **Exodus 30:9**
    - **Deut. 10:17, 18:** *17 For the LORD your God is God of gods, and Lord of lords, a great God, a mighty, and a terrible, which regardeth not persons, nor taketh*

reward: ***18*** *He doth execute the judgment of the fatherless and widow, and loveth the stranger, in giving him food and raiment.* **Deuteronomy 10:17-18**

➢ **Deut. 14:28, 29:** ***28*** *At the end of three years thou shalt bring forth all the tithe of thine increase the same year, and shalt lay it up within thy gates:* ***29*** *And the Levite, (because he hath no part nor inheritance with thee,) and the stranger, and the fatherless, and the widow, which are within thy gates, shall come, and shall eat and be satisfied; that the LORD thy God may bless thee in all the work of thine hand which thou doest.* **Deuteronomy 14:28-29**

➢ **Deut. 16: 10, 14:** *And thou shalt keep the feast of weeks unto the LORD thy God with a tribute of a freewill offering of thine hand, which thou shalt give unto the LORD thy God, according as the LORD thy God hath blessed thee:* **Deuteronomy 16:10** *And thou shalt rejoice in thy feast, thou, and thy son, and thy daughter, and thy manservant, and thy maidservant, and the Levite, the stranger, and the fatherless, and the widow, that are within thy gates.* **Deuteronomy 16:14**

➢ **Deut. 24:17–21:** ***17*** *Thou shalt not pervert the judgment of the stranger, nor of the fatherless; nor take a widow's raiment to pledge:* ***18*** *But thou shalt remember that thou wast a bondman in Egypt, and the LORD thy God redeemed thee thence: therefore I command thee to do this thing.* ***19*** *When thou cuttest down thine harvest in thy field, and hast forgot a sheaf in the field, thou shalt not go again to fetch it: it shall be for the stranger, for the fatherless, and for the widow: that the LORD thy God may bless thee in all the work of thine hands.* ***20*** *When thou beatest thine olive*

CHAPTER 6: SINGLE PARENT FAMILY

tree, thou shalt not go over the boughs again: it shall be for the stranger, for the fatherless, and for the widow. **21** When thou gatherest the grapes of thy vineyard, thou shalt not glean it afterward: it shall be for the stranger, for the fatherless, and for the widow. **Deuteronomy 24:17-21**

➢ **Deut. 27:19:** Cursed be he that perverteth the judgment of the stranger, fatherless, and widow. And all the people shall say, Amen. **Deuteronomy 27:19**

➢ **Psm. 10:14:** Thou hast seen it; for thou beholdest mischief and spite, to requite it with thy hand: the poor committeth himself unto thee; thou art the helper of the fatherless. **Psalms 10:14**

➢ **Psm. 68:5:** A father of the fatherless, and a judge of the widows, is God in his holy habitation. **Psalms 68:5**

➢ **Psm. 146:9:** The LORD preserveth the strangers; he relieveth the fatherless and widow: but the way of the wicked he turneth upside down. **Psalms 146:9**

➢ **Prov. 15:25:** The LORD will destroy the house of the proud: but he will establish the border of the widow. **Proverbs 15:25**

➢ **Isa. 1:17:** Learn to do well; seek judgment, relieve the oppressed, judge the fatherless, plead for the widow. **Isaiah 1:17**

➢ **Jer. 7:6:** If ye oppress not the stranger, the fatherless, and the widow, and shed not innocent blood in this place, neither walk after other gods to your hurt: **Jeremiah 7:6**

➢ **Jer. 49:11:** Leave thy fatherless children, I will preserve them alive; and let thy widows trust in me. **Jeremiah 49:11**

- ➢ **Ezek. 44:22:** *Neither shall they take for their wives a widow, nor her that is put away: but they shall take maidens of the seed of the house of Israel, or a widow that had a priest before.* **Ezekiel 44:22**
- ➢ **Hosea 14:1-3:** *1 O Israel, return unto the LORD thy God; for thou hast fallen by thine iniquity. 2 Take with you words, and turn to the LORD: say unto him, Take away all iniquity, and receive us graciously: so will we render the calves of our lips. 3 Asshur shall not save us; we will not ride upon horses: neither will we say any more to the work of our hands, Ye are our gods: for in thee the fatherless findeth mercy.* **Hosea 14:1-3**
- ➢ **Matt. 23:14:** *Woe unto you, scribes and Pharisees, hypocrites! for ye devour widows' houses, and for a pretence make long prayer: therefore ye shall receive the greater damnation.* **Matthew 23:14**
- ➢ **Mark 12:42, 43:** *42 And there came a certain poor widow, and she threw in two mites, which make a farthing. 43 And he called unto him his disciples, and saith unto them, Verily I say unto you, That this poor widow hath cast more in, than all they which have cast into the treasury:* **Mark 12:42-43**
- ➢ **Luke 7:11:** *And it came to pass the day after, that he went into a city called Nain; and many of his disciples went with him, and much people.* **Luke 7:11**
- ➢ **Acts 6:1:** *And in those days, when the number of the disciples was multiplied, there arose a murmuring of the Grecians against the Hebrews, because their widows were neglected in the daily ministration.* **Acts 6:1**
- ➢ **Acts 9:37, 41:** *And it came to pass in those days, that she was sick, and died: whom when they had washed,*

CHAPTER 6: SINGLE PARENT FAMILY

they laid her in an upper chamber. **Acts 9:37:** *And he gave her his hand, and lifted her up, and when he had called the saints and widows, presented her alive.* **Acts 9:41**

➢ **I Tim. 5:3-5, 9-15:** *3 Honour widows that are widows indeed. 4 But if any widow have children or nephews, let them learn first to shew piety at home, and to requite their parents: for that is good and acceptable before God. 5 Now she that is a widow indeed, and desolate, trusteth in God, and continueth in supplications and prayers night and day.* **1 Timothy 5:3-5** *9 Let not a widow be taken into the number under threescore years old, having been the wife of one man, 10 Well reported of for good works; if she have brought up children, if she have lodged strangers, if she have washed the saints' feet, if she have relieved the afflicted, if she have diligently followed every good work. 11 But the younger widows refuse: for when they have begun to wax wanton against Christ, they will marry; 12 Having damnation, because they have cast off their first faith. 13 And withal they learn to be idle, wandering about from house to house; and not only idle, but tattlers also and busybodies, speaking things which they ought not. 14 I will therefore that the younger women marry, bear children, guide the house, give none occasion to the adversary to speak reproachfully. 15 For some are already turned aside after Satan.* **1 Timothy 5:9-15**

6. Churches can do much to solve the problems in and from the single parent home.

CHAPTER VII

FAMILY IDENTITY

(What makes your family unique?)

A. Origin of Identity

1. Every family unit is made up of so many different factors – often changing, that each family is unique.
2. Two family lines, with all their variety, are blended together into a new family identity.
3. Different family heritage and history combine with value systems, standards, goals, pattern of manners, and relationship with relatives, jobs, reputation, and character. They are mixed with views on government and relationships with the church to make for specific home units.
4. The desired identity of a particular family unit should be chosen and worked on. There should be planning, reasons, and goals for a particular blend. The nature of the identity should be for advantages and not handicaps for members of the family.

B. Heritage and History

1. The Bible cites many cases of how this affected families and society.
2. This involves much of what is actually brought into the marriage – from values, accomplishments, lessons learned, thought patterns, and history – to undergird

decisions, choices, etc. by positive or negative experiences from the past.
3. Research will help us learn of our own past. Honest observation helps us see our present. Planning can give direction for the future.
4. Lines of thought can be woven together to give a helpful picture.

Areas to consider include:

Spiritual	Morality
Intellectual	Emotions
Financial	Service to others

C. Reputation and Character

1. Character is what you are, while reputation is what others think you are or have done. The two are often different. Others can hurt your reputation, but you alone determine what your character will be.
2. Families should seek to build character and only then concern themselves with their reputation. (Some seek to build reputation without building character. They usually fail.)

Areas to consider

Spiritual	Financial
Moral	Work Ethic

D. Goals, Standards, and Values

1. **Values** are what is important (what we value), - the top general areas of our priority list.
2. **Standards** are the minimum acceptable limits of thought, action, and behavior. They should reflect our values. To

lower standards is to decrease the value system of the family.
3. **Goals** are what we aim to accomplish. As a family, they are influenced by our values and standards, and should be rather specific in many areas.
4. Determining our values and establishing our standards will prepare us to set our goals.
5. It can prove healthy to work this out (with many other areas) before a couple marries.
6. There are many areas to consider. *Here are some:*
Spiritual
Raising trained and burdened laborers
Sensitivity to God's leading
Living by faith
Bible knowledge
Prayer life
Concern for missions and ministry
Leadership and followers
Educational
Financial
Job Skills
Morals
Manners
Dress
Separation
Holiness

E. Manners

1. Open or close doors

2. Biblical issue − **I Cor. 15:33:** *Be not deceived: evil communications corrupt good manners.* **1 Corinthians 15:33; Rom. 12:18** *If it be possible, as much as lieth in you, live peaceably with all men.* **Romans 12:18; Phil. 2:4** *Look not every man on his own things, but every man also on the things of others.* **Philippians 2:4;** etc.)

This covers a variety of areas: eating, treatment of others (homes, school, church, work, relatives, friends, strangers, etc.), talking, bodily movements, etc.

F. Relationships with Relatives

1. Each member of the couple marries a whole family, to a lesser degree. The children will have a mixture of many relatives affecting their development.
2. Time to spend with, lines of communication, location of living, holidays spent, etc. all affect the marriage and the family.
3. These relationships can be either supportive or divisive (or mixed). They may open doors or close such financially. They may be a drain or heavy on input.
Guidelines for these relationships involve balance on both sides of the family and, to varying degrees, with a host of relatives, i.e. in-laws, brothers and sisters, nieces and nephews, uncles and aunts, cousins, grandparents, etc.

G. Nature and Attitude Towards Jobs

1. Self-employment vs. working for an employer.
2. Trade or profession in contrast to common laborer.
3. Stick with a job or change often.

4. Future of the job, demands of the job, benefits of the job, etc.
5. Two jobs at once?
6. Work ethics, preparation, and security.

H. Balance with Church and Government

1. Church is not to harm but help the home.
2. Different families in the same church will be different, but not necessarily wrong. Don't judge yourself by others, or vice versa.
3. Function in church, standards, goals, and fellowship will affect the family.
4. Decisions on family attitude towards government need to be made, especially as to how the government may want to affect the family (education, health, finances, abortion, immorality, regulations, immorality, taxes, privacy, etc.).
5. What view and actions will the families take towards church and government relations. *Example:* The Pilgrims.

CHAPTER 7: FAMILY IDENTITY

CHAPTER VIII

SPIRITUAL FUNCTIONS OF THE FAMILY

A. The Home

The home is to nurture and admonish the Leaders and Laborers for the Kingdom of God. **Eph. 6:4** makes it clear that this is the duty primarily of the father. *And, ye fathers, provoke not your children to wrath: but bring them up in the nurture and admonition of the Lord.* **Ephesians 6:4. I Tim. 2:15** shows that the mothers can function here also. **1Ti 2:15** *Notwithstanding she shall be saved in childbearing, if they continue in faith and charity and holiness with sobriety.* (Where does one find even one verse showing such promises, commands, or results for or from a church or synagogue?)

The church (and/or Christian school) in a few hours, cannot do what God assigned the family to accomplish all week. It is not their responsibility nor within their capability. Time will easily demonstrate that any **and** all church (and/or para-church groups) will fail when they try to usurp the home. God will only bless what He has ordained, and not the competition. The church and school should help, and support the home rather than trying to replace it.

B. Training Children Spiritually

    1. Spiritual Goals

CHAPTER 8: SPIRITUAL FUNCTIONS OF THE FAMILY

II Tim. 3:15: *And that from a child thou hast known the holy scriptures, which are able to make thee wise unto salvation through faith which is in Christ Jesus.* **2 Timothy 3:15** *"Know the Holy Scriptures"*

stories	promises
doctrine	warnings
principles	commands

II Tim. 3:15: *"Wise unto salvation"*

saved	evangelistic
faithful	practical application

Psm. 119:9, 11: BETH. *Wherewithal shall a young man cleanse his way? by taking heed thereto according to thy word.* **Psalms 119:9** *Thy word have I hid in mine heart, that I might not sin against thee.* **Psalms 119:11**

memorizing scripture

holy living

2. **Produce Laborers for the Harvest Fields**

knowledgeable	capable
trained	talents developed
burdened	sensitive to God's leading
experienced	

3. **Leaders trained to fill positions as needed**

vision	co-operating
energy & active	humble
consistency	knowledgeable
authority	experience
followers	wisdom
goal setters	love
communication	

C. The Family Spiritual Life

The family spiritual life is made up of many factors. Only as progress is made in these is it likely that the children will develop properly:

1. **Church life and relationship**
    - Faithful to a Biblical church
    - Membership for spiritual protection, provision, and relationship
    - Active in church life as a participant instead of a spectator
    - Consistent in financial support to church and its ministries
    - Learning from its teaching and preaching that growth might occur **(Eph. 4:11-16: 11** *And he gave some, apostles; and some, prophets; and some, evangelists; and some, pastors and teachers;* **12** *For the perfecting of the saints, for the work of the ministry, for the edifying of the body of Christ:* **13** *Till we all come in the unity of the faith, and of the knowledge of the Son of God, unto a perfect man, unto the measure of the stature of the fulness of Christ:* **14** *That we henceforth be no more children, tossed to and fro, and carried about with every wind of doctrine, by the sleight of men, and cunning craftiness, whereby they lie in wait to deceive;* **15** *But speaking the truth in love, may grow up into him in all things, which is the head, even Christ:* **16** *From whom the whole body fitly joined together and compacted by that which every joint supplieth, according to the effectual working in the measure of*

CHAPTER 8: SPIRITUAL FUNCTIONS OF THE FAMILY

every part, maketh increase of the body unto the edifying of itself in love. **Ephesians 4:11-16)**
- ➤ Exhorting each other to greater usefulness and holiness **(Heb. 10:25:** *Not forsaking the assembling of ourselves together, as the manner of some is; but exhorting one another: and so much the more, as ye see the day approaching.* **Hebrews 10:25)**
- ➤ Finding a place of ministry within the local body
- ➤ Co-operating together towards Biblical goals
- ➤ Praying one for another
- ➤ Submitting one to another **(Eph. 5:21:** *Submitting yourselves one to another in the fear of God.* **Ephesians 5:21)**

2. **Attending Bible conferences, special meetings, and camp meetings** for the spiritual growth of the family.
3. **Devotional Life**
   - ➤ Family devotions as the glue to hold the family together and the basis for personal devotions, worship, and prayer together, Bible instruction, and praise.
   - ➤ Personal devotions for each, not as an obligation but as a delight. Each can discover truths, see their prayers answered, and enjoy God's presence.
4. **Prayer Life**
   - ➤ Family together praying for items that affect each other and the family ... as well as the church and nation.
   - ➤ Private praying for particular personal desires as well as for those burdened for. Use of prayer lists is especially effective.

> These should be a way of life, not just moments of prayer, - thus a **Prayer Life**.

5. **Faith Life**
   > Family goals accomplished by faith will teach children early that God is to be trusted. Perhaps faith in the financial realm has been the most used area in recent years. Certainly, there are many others – for example, openings to witness, change of weather or events for the sake of ministry, etc.
   > Personal goals of faith help each to see how they are making spiritual progress. Regular exercise in this area prepares each for operation when particular problems and opportunities show up.

6. **Giving**
   1. Family practice of tithing consistently and then giving more makes for a healthy home as well as bringing God's blessing. Once the pattern is set, the children can easily be instructed to follow it. With encouragement, they will see God's blessing and develop patterns for life-long help from God! It will also steer their hearts towards God as Jesus taught (**Luke 12:23** *The life is more than meat, and the body is more than raiment.* **Luke 12:23**).

7. **Visitation** of the fatherless and the widows in their affliction (**James 1:27:** *Pure religion and undefiled before God and the Father is this, To visit the fatherless and widows in their affliction, and to keep himself unspotted from the world.* **James 1:27**).
   > This helps the family appreciate God for letting them stay together as a family.

CHAPTER 8: SPIRITUAL FUNCTIONS OF THE FAMILY

- ➢ This keeps the family from being self-centered.
- ➢ This ministers to those deprived of a normal home.
- ➢ This is a mark of true religion.
- ➢ This can be a real tool of evangelism.
- ➢ This can help the need to benefit from a functioning family and perhaps overcome their handicaps.

8. **Show Good Works (Eph.2:10; II Tim. 3:17:** *For we are his workmanship, created in Christ Jesus unto good works, which God hath before ordained that we should walk in them.* **Ephesians 2:10;** *That the man of God may be perfect, throughly furnished unto all good works.* **2 Timothy 3:17**).
   - ➢ This is a product of salvation and the inspired scriptures.
   - ➢ Lack of good works throws doubt on both the claims of salvation and the Bible.
   - ➢ The family has many ways to show good works to a dying society.
   - ➢ Volunteer service to help the needy and handicapped work with the young, assist the poor, help with paperwork for the confused, assist others in planning for the future, aid the unemployed in finding work, heal broken homes, encourage the discouraged, reduce crime by reaching potential criminals, teach the work ethic, help students with school work, etc.
   - ➢ God opens doors to those who are prepared. We are furnished by Scripture unto **all** good works.

9. **Family Testimony**
    - Individuals are to be a light.
    - Family units are a cluster of lights that shine to a multitude in a variety of places.
    - A family's identity and spiritual state speak eloquently to neighbors and relatives.
    - Prayer, faith, and good works will open doors for evangelism to the family. The church is the beneficiary of such.

CHAPTER 8: SPIRITUAL FUNCTIONS OF THE FAMILY

CHAPTER IX

EDUCATIONAL FOUNDATIONS

A. Education

1. No education is complete without a thorough knowledge of the Bible.
2. The family often decides to what degree the goal is excellence vs. getting by.
3. The level, direction, nature, and quality of education are a family issue. Even President Clinton, a strong supporter of government-controlled education, believes his family should control his child's education. Therefore, he put Chelsea in the private school of his choice.
4. Education prepares us for life. It lays the foundation for functioning:
    - on the job
    - in the church
    - in adjusting to change
    - in preparing for retirement
    - in enjoying one's job opportunities
    - as a citizen
    - as a voter
    - as an investor
    - in gaining insight to events
    - in preparation for marriage

CHAPTER 9: EDUCATIONAL FOUNDATIONS

B. Learning

1. Learning starts at home. The family is the single biggest factor in a child's ability to learn.
2. God's Word teaches that our ability to learn is not an issue settled at birth, but able to be adjusted by choice. (**Prov. 16:21; 1:17; 1:29; 2:1-6; 9:10; 16:30; 28:5:** *The wise in heart shall be called prudent: and the sweetness of the lips increaseth learning.* **Proverbs 16:21,** *Surely in vain the net is spread in the sight of any bird.* **Proverbs 1:17,** *For that they hated knowledge, and did not choose the fear of the LORD*: **Proverbs 1:29,** *1 My son, if thou wilt receive my words, and hide my commandments with thee; 2 So that thou incline thine ear unto wisdom, and apply thine heart to understanding; 3 Yea, if thou criest after knowledge, and liftest up thy voice for understanding; 4 If thou seekest her as silver, and searchest for her as for hid treasures; 5 Then shalt thou understand the fear of the LORD, and find the knowledge of God. 6 For the LORD giveth wisdom: out of his mouth cometh knowledge and understanding.* **Proverbs 2:1-6,** *The fear of the LORD is the beginning of wisdom: and the knowledge of the holy is understanding.* **Proverbs 9:10,** *He shutteth his eyes to devise froward things: moving his lips he bringeth evil to pass.* **Proverbs 16:30,** *Evil men understand not judgment: but they that seek the LORD understand all things.* **Proverbs 28:5**)
3. Learning must be valued, and the value is home established. (**Prov. 2:2, 4; 3:13-15; 8:10, 11, 19; 16:16; 23:23:** *So that thou incline thine ear unto wisdom, and apply thine heart to understanding;* **Proverbs 2:2,** *If thou seekest her as silver, and searchest for her as for hid*

treasures; **Proverbs 2:4, 13** *Happy is the man that findeth wisdom, and the man that getteth understanding.* ***14*** *For the merchandise of it is better than the merchandise of silver, and the gain thereof than fine gold.* ***15*** *She is more precious than rubies: and all the things thou canst desire are not to be compared unto her.* **Proverbs 3:13-15, 10** *Receive my instruction, and not silver; and knowledge rather than choice gold.* ***11*** *For wisdom is better than rubies; and all the things that may be desired are not to be compared to it.* **Proverbs 8:10-11,** *My fruit is better than gold, yea, than fine gold; and my revenue than choice silver.* **Proverbs 8:19,** *How much better is it to get wisdom than gold! and to get understanding rather to be chosen than silver!* **Proverbs 16:16,** *Buy the truth, and sell it not; also wisdom, and instruction, and understanding.* **Proverbs 23:23**)

4. Learning requires proper attitudes. Families should work at encouraging these attitudes. (**Prov. 3:5, 7; 11:2; 9:2-5; 16:21; 8:17; 12:1; 13:16, 20:** *Trust in the LORD with all thine heart; and lean not unto thine own understanding.* **Proverbs 3:5,** *Be not wise in thine own eyes: fear the LORD, and depart from evil.* **Proverbs 3:7,** *When pride cometh, then cometh shame: but with the lowly is wisdom.* **Proverbs 11:2, 2** *She hath killed her beasts; she hath mingled her wine; she hath also furnished her table.* ***3*** *She hath sent forth her maidens: she crieth upon the highest places of the city,* ***4*** *Whoso is simple, let him turn in hither: as for him that wanteth understanding, she saith to him,* ***5*** *Come, eat of my bread, and drink of the wine which I have mingled.* **Proverbs 9:2-5,** *The wise in heart shall be called prudent: and the sweetness of the lips increaseth learning.* **Proverbs 16:21,** *I love them that love*

me; and those that seek me early shall find me. **Proverbs 8:17,** Whoso loveth instruction loveth knowledge: but he that hateth reproof is brutish. **Proverbs 12:1,** Every prudent man dealeth with knowledge: but a fool layeth open his folly. **Proverbs 13:16,** He that walketh with wise men shall be wise: but a companion of fools shall be destroyed. **Proverbs 13:20**).

5. God has established **five** Laws of Learning:
   i. Hear

   (**Prov. 1:5; 5:7; 13:1; 15:32; 4:10; 19:20; 23:19; 8:33:** A wise man will hear, and will increase learning; and a man of understanding shall attain unto wise counsels: **Proverbs 1:5,** Hear me now therefore, O ye children, and depart not from the words of my mouth. **Proverbs 5:7,** A wise son heareth his father's instruction: but a scorner heareth not rebuke. **Proverbs 13:1,** He that refuseth instruction despiseth his own soul: but he that heareth reproof getteth understanding. **Proverbs 15:32,** Hear, O my son, and receive my sayings; and the years of thy life shall be many. **Proverbs 4:10,** Hear counsel, and receive instruction, that thou mayest be wise in thy latter end. **Proverbs 19:20,** Hear thou, my son, and be wise, and guide thine heart in the way. **Proverbs 23:19,** Hear instruction, and be wise, and refuse it not. **Proverbs 8:33**)

   ii. Pay Attention

   (**Prov. 4:1; 20: 5:1:** Hear, ye children, the instruction of a father, and attend to know understanding. **Proverbs 4:1,** My son, attend to my words; incline thine ear unto my sayings. **Proverbs**

4:20, *My son, attend unto my wisdom, and bow thine ear to my understanding:* **Proverbs 5:1**)

iii. Desire to Learn – Seek Knowledge
(**Prov. 8:17; 15:14; 17:16; 18:1, 2; 4:5, 7:** *I love them that love me; and those that seek me early shall find me.* **Proverbs 8:17,** *The heart of him that hath understanding seeketh knowledge: but the mouth of fools feedeth on foolishness.* **Proverbs 15:14,** *Wherefore is there a price in the hand of a fool to get wisdom, seeing he hath no heart to it?* **Proverbs 17:16, 1** *Through desire a man, having separated himself, seeketh and intermeddleth with all wisdom. 2 A fool hath no delight in understanding, but that his heart may discover itself.* **Proverbs 18:1-2,** *Get wisdom, get understanding: forget it not; neither decline from the words of my mouth.* **Proverbs 4:5,** *Wisdom is the principal thing; therefore get wisdom: and with all thy getting get understanding.* **Proverbs 4:7**)

iv. Apply Yourself
(**Prov. 22:17; 23:12; 2:2, 3:** *Bow down thine ear, and hear the words of the wise, and apply thine heart unto my knowledge.* **Proverbs 22:17,** *Apply thine heart unto instruction, and thine ears to the words of knowledge.* **Proverbs 23:12, 2** *So that thou incline thine ear unto wisdom, and apply thine heart to understanding; 3 Yea, if thou criest after knowledge, and liftest up thy voice for understanding;* **Proverbs 2:2-3**)

v. Get It and Keep It

(**Prov: 4:5, 13; 10:14; 4:4, 21; 6:20, 21; 7:1-3:** *Get wisdom, get understanding: forget it not; neither decline from the words of my mouth.* **Proverbs 4:5,** *Take fast hold of instruction; let her not go: keep her; for she is thy life.* **Proverbs 4:13,** *Wise men lay up knowledge: but the mouth of the foolish is near destruction.* **Proverbs 10:14,** *He taught me also, and said unto me, Let thine heart retain my words: keep my commandments, and live.* **Proverbs 4:4,** *Let them not depart from thine eyes; keep them in the midst of thine heart.* **Proverbs 4:21, 1** *My son, keep my words, and lay up my commandments with thee. 2 Keep my commandments, and live; and my law as the apple of thine eye. 3 Bind them upon thy fingers, write them upon the table of thine heart.* **Proverbs 7:1-3)**

6. There are **six** methods of teaching given in Proverbs

   i. Use of Proverbs

   (**Prov. 1:1-4 1** *The proverbs of Solomon the son of David, king of Israel; 2 To know wisdom and instruction; to perceive the words of understanding; 3 To receive the instruction of wisdom, justice, and judgment, and equity; 4 To give subtilty to the simple, to the young man knowledge and discretion.* **Proverbs 1:1-4)**

   ii. Reproof

   (**Prov. 19:25; 15:32:** *Smite a scorner, and the simple will beware: and reprove one that hath understanding, and he will understand knowledge.* **Proverbs 19:25,** *He that refuseth instruction* despiseth his own soul: but he that heareth reproof getteth understanding. **Proverbs 15:32**)

iii. Rod

(**Prov. 29:15:** *The rod and reproof give wisdom: but a child left to himself bringeth his mother to shame.* **Proverbs 29:15**)

iv. Fear of the Lord

(**Prov. 1:7:** *The fear of the LORD is the beginning of knowledge: but fools despise wisdom and instruction.* **Proverbs 1:7**)

v. Receive words spoken

(**Prov. 2:1:** *My son, if thou wilt receive my words, and hide my commandments with thee;* **Proverbs 2:1**)

vi. Instruction given

(**Prov. 4:1, 13: 9:9; 13:1; 19:20, 27; 21:11, 23:23; 8:33:** *Hear, ye children, the instruction of a father, and attend to know understanding.* **Proverbs 4:1,** *Take fast hold of instruction; let her not go: keep her; for she is thy life.* **Proverbs 4:13,** *Give instruction to a wise man, and he will be yet wiser: teach a just man, and he will increase in learning.* **Proverbs 9:9,** *A wise son heareth his father's instruction: but a scorner heareth not rebuke.* **Proverbs 13:1,** *Hear counsel, and receive instruction, that thou mayest be wise in thy latter end.* **Proverbs 19:20,** *Cease, my son, to hear the instruction that causeth to err from the words of knowledge.* **Proverbs 19:27,** *When the scorner is punished, the simple is made wise: and when the wise is instructed, he receiveth knowledge.*

CHAPTER 9: EDUCATIONAL FOUNDATIONS

> **Proverbs 21:11,** *Buy the truth, and sell it not; also wisdom, and instruction, and understanding.* **Proverbs 23:23,** *Hear instruction, and be wise, and refuse it not.* **Proverbs 8:33**)

C. Reading

1. Reading is the single biggest factor in education. Reading allows one to continue and develop their education in most any direction to most any end.
2. Reading is foundational to good communication and the ability to write. By-passing reading handicaps the education and usefulness of the individual.
3. The desire to read is more easily caught than taught. Seeing parents read often instills a desire to read in the child. Reading skills and mastery of material usually don't just happen, but are developed by plan.
4. A desire to read and a joy from it can often be developed by some family reading. Father or mother reading to children not only teaches what is being read, but also encourages them to read to each other, etc.
5. A variety of good reading can be found in newspapers, magazines, booklets, books, etc.
6. Studies have shown that homes with 100 or more books have students doing better than those from homes of less than 50 books. Also, students that read more and watch TV less do better.

D. Time Usage

1. To properly operate a family and best raise children will obviously require a careful usage of time.
2. Time is of greater value than money, as we can always earn more, but our time is limited.
3. God teaches us to be *"Redeeming the time."* (**Col. 4:5; Eph. 5:15, 16:** *Walk in wisdom toward them that are without, redeeming the time.* **Colossians 4:5;** *15 See then that ye walk circumspectly, not as fools, but as wise, 16 Redeeming the time, because the days are evil.* **Ephesians 5:15-16**)
4. Time is to be spent in such a way as to leave a story worth telling (**Psalm. 90:9:** *For all our days are passed away in thy wrath: we spend our years as a tale that is told.* **Psalms 90:9**). We are to number the days, and may live 70-80 years (**Psalm. 90:10, 12:** *The days of our years are threescore years and ten; and if by reason of strength they be fourscore years, yet is their strength labour and sorrow; for it is soon cut off, and we fly away.* **Psalms 90:10,** *So teach us to number our days, that we may apply our hearts unto wisdom.* **Psalms 90:12**). Seventy years is 25,550 days, while 80 years equals 29,200 days. Every 30 years is approximately 11,000 days. This is not long to live, and we must learn how to use the time properly.
5. Wasting or investing our life is a day-by-day process. At home, we can impress each other with the need to rightly use each day properly. Every the day is spent an hour at a time (perhaps 600,000 in a lifetime), and must be watched over lest it be lost.

Each will probably sleep 200,000 hours, work 100,000 hours, and eat during 50,000 hours. That leaves a maximum of only 250,000 hours for all other activities, including school (20,000 hours), travel, recreation, chores, vacations, childhood, hobbies, serving God etc.

6. Time management involves:
    ➢ setting priorities
    ➢ setting goals
    ➢ planning and organization
    ➢ accountability
    ➢ problem solving
    ➢ evaluation

(For a greater in-depth study of time usage, see "Redeeming the Time.")

CHAPTER X

FINANCIAL OPERATIONS

A. Importance

1. Proper training will prepare children for usefulness to God, the Church, and their nation in the financial realm. Failure to train will handicap the children in their giving, paying their bills, paying taxes, and helping develop local and national economics.
2. Support of the parents in their old age may be meager if this area is not properly taught.
3. This should include proper practice as well as thorough instruction. The health of the home unit is often tied to its finances. Money trouble is the number one root cause of divorce.

B. Poverty – Its Causes and Cures

1. The righteous will seek, find, and consider the causes of poverty. (**Prov. 29:7:** *The voice of the LORD divideth the flames of fire.* **Psalms 29:7**)
2. While **most poverty is chosen**, some is beyond an individual's control. For example:

Sickness	Family death	Taxes
Disasters	Weather	War
Economy	Handicaps	Health
Government	God's Judgment	

3. Finding the cause(s) is a major step towards finding the cure.
4. Most causes of poverty can be dealt with:

CHAPTER 10: FINANCIAL OPERATIONS

1. Dealing with greedy people (**Prov. 1:17-19:** *17 Surely in vain the net is spread in the sight of any bird. 18 And they lay wait for their own blood; they lurk privily for their own lives. 19 So are the ways of every one that is greedy of gain; which taketh away the life of the owners thereof.* **Proverbs 1:17-19**)
2. Too much sleep (**Prov. 6:10,11; 20:13; 23:21; 24:33, 34:** *10 Yet a little sleep, a little slumber, a little folding of the hands to sleep: 11 So shall thy poverty come as one that travelleth, and thy want as an armed man.* **Proverbs 6:10-11,** *Love not sleep, lest thou come to poverty; open thine eyes, and thou shalt be satisfied with bread.* **Proverbs 20:13,** *For the drunkard and the glutton shall come to poverty: and drowsiness shall clothe a man with rags.* **Proverbs 23:21,** *33 Yet a little sleep, a little slumber, a little folding of the hands to sleep: 34 So shall thy poverty come as one that travelleth; and thy want as an armed man.* **Proverbs 24:33-34**)
3. Traveling (**Prov. 6:11; 24:34:** *So shall thy poverty come as one that travelleth, and thy want as an armed man.* **Proverbs 6:11,** *So shall thy poverty come as one that travelleth; and thy want as an armed man.* **Proverbs 24:34**)
4. Loose living (**Prov. 6:26; 5:3-10; 29:3; 23:27; Luke 15:30:** *For by means of a whorish woman a man is brought to a piece of bread: and the adulteress will hunt for the precious life.* **Proverbs 6:26**)
5. Living wickedly (**Prov. 10:2, 3:** *2 Treasures of wickedness profit nothing: but righteousness delivereth from death. 3 The LORD will not suffer the

soul of the righteous to famish: but he casteth away the substance of the wicked. **Proverbs 10:2-3**)

6. Dealing with a slack hand (**Prov. 10:4:** *He becometh poor that dealeth with a slack hand: but the hand of the diligent maketh rich.* **Proverbs 10:4**)

7. Weak national defense (**Prov. 10:15, 18:11:** *The rich man's wealth is his strong city: the destruction of the poor is their poverty.* **Proverbs 10:15,** *The rich man's wealth is his strong city, and as an high wall in his own conceit.* **Proverbs 18:11**)

8. Stinginess in giving (**Prov. 11:24; 3:9, 10:** *There is that scattereth, and yet increaseth; and there is that withholdeth more than is meet, but it tendeth to poverty.* **Proverbs 11:24, 9** *Honour the LORD with thy substance, and with the firstfruits of all thine increase: 10 So shall thy barns be filled with plenty, and thy presses shall burst out with new wine.* **Proverbs 3:9-10**)

9. Vanity (**Prov. 13:11:** *Wealth gotten by vanity shall be diminished: but he that gathereth by labour shall increase.* **Proverbs 13:11**)

10. Refusing instructions (**Prov. 13:18, 8:** Poverty and shame *shall be to* him that refuseth instruction: but he that regardeth reproof shall be honoured. **Proverbs 13:18,** *The ransom of a man's life are his riches: but the poor heareth not rebuke.* **Proverbs 13:8**)

11. Talking instead of laboring (**Prov. 14:23:** *In all labour there is profit: but the talk of the lips tendeth only to penury.* **Proverbs 14:23**)

12. Wasteful (**Prov. 18:9,** *He also that is slothful in his work is brother to him that is a great waster.* **Proverbs 18:9**)

CHAPTER 10: FINANCIAL OPERATIONS

13. Slothful (**Prov. 18:9; 19:15; 12:24, 27; 13:4; 20:4; 21:25; 24:30-32; 26:13-16:** *He also that is slothful in his work is brother to him that is a great waster.* **Proverbs 18:9,** *Slothfulness casteth into a deep sleep; and an idle soul shall suffer hunger.* **Proverbs 19:15,** *The hand of the diligent shall bear rule: but the slothful shall be under tribute.* **Proverbs 12:24,** *The slothful man roasteth not that which he took in hunting: but the substance of a diligent man is precious.* **Proverbs 12:27,** *The sluggard will not plow by reason of the cold; therefore shall he beg in harvest, and have nothing.* **Proverbs 20:4,** *The desire of the slothful killeth him; for his hands refuse to labour.* **Proverbs 21:25, 30** *I went by the field of the slothful, and by the vineyard of the man void of understanding;* **31** *And, lo, it was all grown over with thorns, and nettles had covered the face thereof, and the stone wall thereof was broken down.* **32** *Then I saw, and considered it well: I looked upon it, and received instruction.* **Proverbs 24:30-32, 13** *The slothful man saith, There is a lion in the way; a lion is in the streets.* **14** *As the door turneth upon his hinges, so doth the slothful upon his bed.* **15** *The slothful hideth his hand in his bosom; it grieveth him to bring it again to his mouth.* **16** *The sluggard is wiser in his own conceit than seven men that can render a reason.* **Proverbs 26:13-16**)

14. Ignoring the needs of the poor (**Prov. 21:13; 28:27; 19:17; Ezek. 16:48-50:** *Whoso stoppeth his ears at the cry of the poor, he also shall cry himself, but shall not be heard.* **Proverbs 21:13,** *He that giveth unto the poor shall not lack: but he that hideth his eyes shall have many a curse.* **Proverbs 28:27,** *He that hath pity*

upon the poor lendeth unto the LORD; and that which he hath given will he pay him again. **Proverbs 19:17, 48** *As I live, saith the Lord GOD, Sodom thy sister hath not done, she nor her daughters, as thou hast done, thou and thy daughters.* **49** *Behold, this was the iniquity of thy sister Sodom, pride, fulness of bread, and abundance of idleness was in her and in her daughters, neither did she strengthen the hand of the poor and needy.* **50** *And they were haughty, and committed abomination before me: therefore I took them away as I saw good.* **Ezekiel 16:48-50**)

15. Love of pleasures (**Prov. 21:17:** *He that loveth pleasure shall be a poor man: he that loveth wine and oil shall not be rich.* **Proverbs 21:17**)
16. Spending all you get (**Prov. 21:20:** *There is treasure to be desired and oil in the dwelling of the wise; but a foolish man spendeth it up.* **Proverbs 21:20**)
17. Borrowing money (**Prov. 22:7:** *The rich ruleth over the poor, and the borrower is servant to the lender.* **Proverbs 22:7**)
18. Oppressing the poor (**Prov. 22:16:** *He that oppresseth the poor to increase his riches, and he that giveth to the rich, shall surely come to want.* **Proverbs 22:16**)
19. Giving gifts to the rich (**Prov. 22:16: see the verse above.**)
20. Drunkenness (**Prov. 23:21; 21:17:** *For the drunkard and the glutton shall come to poverty: and drowsiness shall clothe a man with rags.* **Proverbs 23:21,** *He that loveth pleasure shall be a poor man: he that loveth wine and oil shall not be rich.* **Proverbs 21:17**)

CHAPTER 10: FINANCIAL OPERATIONS

21. Gluttony (**Prov. 23:21:** *For the drunkard and the glutton shall come to poverty: and drowsiness shall clothe a man with rags.* **Proverbs 23:21**)
22. Following vain people (**Prov. 28:19; 12:11:** *He that tilleth his land shall have plenty of bread: but he that followeth after vain persons shall have poverty enough.* **Proverbs 28:19,** *He that tilleth his land shall be satisfied with bread: but he that followeth vain persons is void of understanding.* **Proverbs 12:11**)
23. Get-rich-quick schemes (**Prov. 28:22; 13:7; 20:21; 15:27; 21:5; 28:20:** *He that hasteth to be rich hath an evil eye, and considereth not that poverty shall come upon him.* **Proverbs 28:22,** *There is that maketh himself rich, yet hath nothing: there is that maketh himself poor, yet hath great riches.* **Proverbs 13:7,** *An inheritance may be gotten hastily at the beginning; but the end thereof shall not be blessed.* **Proverbs 20:21,** *The lips of the wise disperse knowledge: but the heart of the foolish doeth not so.* **Proverbs 15:7,** *The thoughts of the diligent tend only to plenteousness; but of every one that is hasty only to want.* **Proverbs 21:5,** *A faithful man shall abound with blessings: but he that maketh haste to be rich shall not be innocent.* **Proverbs 28:20**)

5. Proper practices will safeguard family finances.
6. Proper teaching will prepare children for life.

C. Working

1. Developing a work ethic in parents will usually help the children (Laziness is natural and easily learned).

2. Work is to be with great effort ("sweat of the face") because of the curse of sin. (**Gen. 3:17-19: 17** *And unto Adam he said, Because thou hast hearkened unto the voice of thy wife, and hast eaten of the tree, of which I commanded thee, saying, Thou shalt not eat of it: cursed is the ground for thy sake; in sorrow shalt thou eat of it all the days of thy life;* **18** *Thorns also and thistles shall it bring forth to thee; and thou shalt eat the herb of the field;* **19** *In the sweat of thy face shalt thou eat bread, till thou return unto the ground; for out of it wast thou taken: for dust thou art, and unto dust shalt thou return.* **Genesis 3:17-19**) To avoid hard labor is to avoid God's reminder and violate God's Word (**Prov. 13:11; 20:4; 22:13; 24:33, 34; 28:19:** *Wealth gotten by vanity shall be diminished: but he that gathereth by labour shall increase.* **Proverbs 13:11,** *The sluggard will not plow by reason of the cold; therefore shall he beg in harvest, and have nothing.* **Proverbs 20:4,** *The slothful man saith, There is a lion without, I shall be slain in the streets.* **Proverbs 22:13, 33** *Yet a little sleep, a little slumber, a little folding of the hands to sleep:* **34** *So shall thy poverty come as one that travelleth; and thy want as an armed man.* **Proverbs 24:33-34,** *He that tilleth his land shall have plenty of bread: but he that followeth after vain persons shall have poverty enough.* **Proverbs 28:19**)
3. Work is to be six full days a week (**Ex. 20:9:** *Six days shalt thou labour, and do all thy work:* **Exodus 20:9**). This would amount to 60-72 hours a week, allowing for work around home and a 40-hour work week; this allows plenty of time for developing a second income, some self-employment, or volunteer work.

CHAPTER 10: FINANCIAL OPERATIONS

4. Hard and long work will always pay off. (**Prov. 6:6-11; 10:4, 5:** *6 Go to the ant, thou sluggard; consider her ways, and be wise: 7 Which having no guide, overseer, or ruler, 8 Provideth her meat in the summer, and gathereth her food in the harvest. 9 How long wilt thou sleep, O sluggard? when wilt thou arise out of thy sleep? 10 Yet a little sleep, a little slumber, a little folding of the hands to sleep: 11 So shall thy poverty come as one that travelleth, and thy want as an armed man.* **Proverbs 6:6-11,** *4 He becometh poor that dealeth with a slack hand: but the hand of the diligent maketh rich. 5 He that gathereth in summer is a wise son: but he that sleepeth in harvest is a son that causeth shame.* **Proverbs 10:4-5**)

5. We should work quietly to provide for our own needs (and others). Those who **won't** (not can't), should not eat. Work is to produce for us, not welfare, gambling, stealing, etc. (**II Thess. 3:10-12; Prov. 1:10-15:** *10 For even when we were with you, this we commanded you, that if any would not work, neither should he eat. 11 For we hear that there are some which walk among you disorderly, working not at all, but are busybodies. 12 Now them that are such we command and exhort by our Lord Jesus Christ, that with quietness they work, and eat their own bread.* **2 Thessalonians 3:10-12,** *10 My son, if sinners entice thee, consent thou not. 11 If they say, Come with us, let us lay wait for blood, let us lurk privily for the innocent without cause: 12 Let us swallow them up alive as the grave; and whole, as those that go down into the pit: 13 We shall find all precious substance, we shall fill our houses with spoil: 14 Cast in thy lot among us; let us all have one purse: 15 My son, walk not thou in the way with them; refrain thy foot from their path:* **Proverbs 1:10-15**)

D. Business

1. The concept of being an employee of others always had the concept of slavery or servitude (servant) until recently.
2. **I Thess. 4:11:** teaches the need to have some business of our own. *And that ye study to be quiet, and to do your own business, and to work with your own hands, as we commanded you;* **1 Thessalonians 4:11**
3. Businesses, concepts, skills, and opportunities can be passed on to the next generation.
4. The Bible has dozens of scriptures teaching how to operate with multitudes of examples to learn from.

E. Borrowing, Co-signing, Lending, Interest

1. Borrowing makes for bondage (**Prov. 22:7:** *The rich ruleth over the poor, and the borrower is servant to the lender.* **Proverbs 22:7**). We end up working for the lender.
2. We should never borrow from other nations (**Deut. 15:6:** *For the LORD thy God blesseth thee, as he promised thee: and thou shalt lend unto many nations, but thou shalt not borrow; and thou shalt reign over many nations, but they shall not reign over thee.* **Deuteronomy 15:6**).
3. Debt should only be for essentials (taxes, food, etc. (**Neh. 5:1-4: 1** *And there was a great cry of the people and of their wives against their brethren the Jews.* **2** *For there were that said, We, our sons, and our daughters, are many: therefore we take up corn for them, that we may eat, and*

live. 3 Some also there were that said, We have mortgaged our lands, vineyards, and houses, that we might buy corn, because of the dearth. 4 There were also that said, We have borrowed money for the king's tribute, and that upon our lands and vineyards. **Nehemiah 5:1-4**).

4. Never borrow beyond your assets (**Rom. 13:8:** *Owe no man any thing, but to love one another: for he that loveth another hath fulfilled the law.* **Romans 13:8**). It is sinful not to pay your debts (**Psm. 37:21,** *The wicked borroweth, and payeth not again: but the righteous sheweth mercy, and giveth.* **Psalms 37:21**).

5. Co-signing is borrowing without getting anything but debt. It is a sign of ignorance and it is to be avoided (**Prov. 17:18; 20:16: 27:13; 11:15; 22:26:** *A man void of understanding striketh hands, and becometh surety in the presence of his friend.* **Proverbs 17:18,** *Take his garment that is surety for a stranger: and take a pledge of him for a strange woman.* **Proverbs 20:16,** *I had fainted, unless I had believed to see the goodness of the LORD in the land of the living.* **Psalms 27:13,** *He that is surety for a stranger shall smart for it: and he that hateth suretiship is sure.* **Proverbs 11:15,** *Be not thou one of them that strike hands, or of them that are sureties for debts.* **Proverbs 22:26**). If one is already involved, it must be faced (**Prov. 6:1-5:** *1 My son, if thou be surety for thy friend, if thou hast stricken thy hand with a stranger, 2 Thou art snared with the words of thy mouth, thou art taken with the words of thy mouth. 3 Do this now, my son, and deliver thyself, when thou art come into the hand of thy friend; go, humble thyself, and make sure thy friend. 4 Give not sleep to thine eyes, nor slumber to thine eyelids. 5 Deliver thyself as a roe from the*

hand of the hunter, and as a bird from the hand of the fowler. **Proverbs 6:1-5**).

6. Lending is the ability to help or destroy by loaning. It changes the relationships between friends (**Prov. 22:7:** *The rich ruleth over the poor, and the borrower is servant to the lender.* **Proverbs 22:7**) God lays down rules for loans:

Deut. 15:1-11   **Prov. 19:17**
Psm. 112:5   **Ex. 22:25-27**
Deut. 24:6, 10-13   **Deut. 23:19, 20**
Matt. 5:42   **Lev. 25:36, 37**
Luke 6:34, 35 (SEE THE TABLE OF SCRIPTURES BELOW)

| *1 At the end of every seven years thou shalt make a release. 2 And this is the manner of the release: Every creditor that lendeth ought unto his neighbour shall release it; he shall not exact it of his neighbour, or of his brother; because it is called the LORD'S release. 3 Of a foreigner thou mayest exact it again: but that which is thine with thy brother thine hand shall release; 4 Save when there shall be no poor among you; for the LORD shall greatly bless thee in the land which the LORD thy God giveth thee for an inheritance to possess it: 5* | *He that hath pity upon the poor lendeth unto the LORD; and that which he hath given will he pay him again.* **Proverbs 19:17** |

CHAPTER 10: FINANCIAL OPERATIONS

Only if thou carefully hearken unto the voice of the LORD thy God, to observe to do all these commandments which I command thee this day. **6** *For the LORD thy God blesseth thee, as he promised thee: and thou shalt lend unto many nations, but thou shalt not borrow; and thou shalt reign over many nations, but they shall not reign over thee.* **7** *If there be among you a poor man of one of thy brethren within any of thy gates in thy land which the LORD thy God giveth thee, thou shalt not harden thine heart, nor shut thine hand from thy poor brother:* **Deuteronomy 15:1-7**	
A good man sheweth favour, and lendeth: he will guide his affairs with discretion. **Psalms 112:5**	**25** *If thou lend money to any of my people that is poor by thee, thou shalt not be to him as an usurer, neither shalt thou lay upon him usury.* **26** *If thou at all take thy neighbour's raiment to pledge, thou shalt deliver it unto him by that the sun goeth down:* **27** *For that is his covering only, it is his raiment for his skin: wherein shall he*

	sleep? and it shall come to pass, when he crieth unto me, that I will hear; for I am gracious. **Exodus 22:25-27**
No man shall take the nether or the upper millstone to pledge: for he taketh a man's life to pledge. **Deuteronomy 24:6, 10** *When thou dost lend thy brother any thing, thou shalt not go into his house to fetch his pledge.* **11** *Thou shalt stand abroad, and the man to whom thou dost lend shall bring out the pledge abroad unto thee.* **12** *And if the man be poor, thou shalt not sleep with his pledge:* **13** *In any case thou shalt deliver him the pledge again when the sun goeth down, that he may sleep in his own raiment, and bless thee: and it shall be righteousness unto thee before the LORD thy God.* **Deuteronomy 24:10-13**	**19** *Thou shalt not lend upon usury to thy brother; usury of money, usury of victuals, usury of any thing that is lent upon usury:* **20** *Unto a stranger thou mayest lend upon usury; but unto thy brother thou shalt not lend upon usury: that the LORD thy God may bless thee in all that thou settest thine hand to in the land whither thou goest to possess it.* **Deuteronomy 23:19-20**
Give to him that asketh thee, and from him that would borrow of thee turn not thou away. **Matthew 5:42**	**36** *Take thou no usury of him, or increase: but fear thy God; that thy brother may live with thee.* **37** *Thou shalt not give him thy money upon usury, nor lend him thy victuals for*

CHAPTER 10: FINANCIAL OPERATIONS

	increase. **Leviticus 25:36-37**
34 And if ye lend to them of whom ye hope to receive, what thank have ye? for sinners also lend to sinners, to receive as much again. 35 But love ye your enemies, and do good, and lend, hoping for nothing again; and your reward shall be great, and ye shall be the children of the Highest: for he is kind unto the unthankful and to the evil. **Luke 6:34-35**	

7. Interest should never become usury (**Neh. 5:4-13; Psm. 15:1-5; Prov. 28:8; Jer. 15:10; Ezek. 18:10-17; Ezek. 22:12, 13:** *4 There were also that said, We have borrowed money for the king's tribute, and that upon our lands and vineyards. 5 Yet now our flesh is as the flesh of our brethren, our children as their children: and, lo, we bring into bondage our sons and our daughters to be servants, and some of our daughters are brought unto bondage already: neither is it in our power to redeem them; for other men have our lands and vineyards. 6 And I was very angry when I heard their cry and these words. 7 Then I consulted with myself, and I rebuked the nobles, and the rulers, and said unto them, Ye exact usury, every one of his brother. And I set a great assembly against them. 8 And I said unto them, We after our ability have redeemed our brethren the Jews, which were sold unto the heathen; and will ye even sell your brethren? or shall they be sold unto*

us? Then held they their peace, and found nothing to answer. 9 Also I said, It is not good that ye do: ought ye not to walk in the fear of our God because of the reproach of the heathen our enemies? 10 I likewise, and my brethren, and my servants, might exact of them money and corn: I pray you, let us leave off this usury. 11 Restore, I pray you, to them, even this day, their lands, their vineyards, their oliveyards, and their houses, also the hundredth part of the money, and of the corn, the wine, and the oil, that ye exact of them. 12 Then said they, We will restore them, and will require nothing of them; so will we do as thou sayest. Then I called the priests, and took an oath of them, that they should do according to this promise. 13 Also I shook my lap, and said, So God shake out every man from his house, and from his labour, that performeth not this promise, even thus be he shaken out, and emptied. And all the congregation said, Amen, and praised the LORD. And the people did according to this promise. **Nehemiah 5:4-13,** *He that by usury and unjust gain increaseth his substance, he shall gather it for him that will pity the poor.* **Proverbs 28:8,** *Woe is me, my mother, that thou hast borne me a man of strife and a man of contention to the whole earth! I have neither lent on usury, nor men have lent to me on usury; yet every one of them doth curse me.* **Jeremiah 15:10, 10** *If he beget a son that is a robber, a shedder of blood, and that doeth the like to any one of these things,* **11** *And that doeth not any of those duties, but even hath eaten upon the mountains, and defiled his neighbour's wife,* **12** *Hath oppressed the poor and needy, hath spoiled by violence, hath not restored the pledge, and hath lifted up his eyes to the idols, hath committed abomination,* **13** *Hath given forth upon usury, and hath taken increase: shall he then* *live? he shall not live: he hath done all these abominations; he shall surely die; his blood shall be upon him.* **14** *Now, lo, if he beget a son, that seeth all his father's sins which he hath done, and considereth, and doeth not such like,* **15** *That hath not eaten upon the mountains, neither hath lifted up his eyes to the idols of the house of Israel, hath not defiled his neighbour's wife,* **16** *Neither hath oppressed any, hath not withholden the pledge, neither hath spoiled by violence, but hath given his bread to the hungry, and hath covered the naked with a garment,* **17** *That hath taken off his hand from the poor, that hath not received usury nor increase, hath executed my judgments, hath walked in my statutes; he shall not die for the iniquity of his father, he shall surely live.* **Ezekiel 18:10-17, 12** *In thee have they taken gifts to shed blood; thou hast taken usury and increase, and thou hast greedily gained of thy neighbours by extortion, and hast forgotten me, saith the Lord GOD.* **13** *Behold, therefore I have smitten mine hand at thy dishonest gain which thou hast made, and at thy blood which hath been in the midst of thee.* **Ezekiel 22:12-13**)

    8. Interest rates should involve consideration of:
- Cost of getting dollars before you earn them
- Profit for the owners of the dollars
- Amount to be given for owners' lost opportunities to have used their own money to make money
- Amount for inflation
- Amount for the element of risk

F. Priorities

1. Consider your family identity, values, and goals.

2. Use of finances can become a powerful tool in the present or the future.
3. Money handling should be planned rather than just happening.

G. Savings and Investments

1. Savings are not a lack of trust in God, but rather, an act of obedience. It is preparing for what God told us is going to come (**Prov. 30:24, 25: 6:6-11; 10:4,5: 21:5; 12:11; 28:19, 20; 12:27; 13:11; 20:4; 21:20; 22:1-4, 7; 24:27; 31:13, 14, 16, 21, 24:** *24 There be four things which are little upon the earth, but they are exceeding wise: 25 The ants are a people not strong, yet they prepare their meat in the summer;* **Proverbs 30:24-25,** *6 Go to the ant, thou sluggard; consider her ways, and be wise: 7 Which having no guide, overseer, or ruler, 8 Provideth her meat in the summer, and gathereth her food in the harvest. 9 How long wilt thou sleep, O sluggard? when wilt thou arise out of thy sleep? 10 Yet a little sleep, a little slumber, a little folding of the hands to sleep: 11 So shall thy poverty come as one that travelleth, and thy want as an armed man.* **Proverbs 6:6-11,** *4 He becometh poor that dealeth with a slack hand: but the hand of the diligent maketh rich. 5 He that gathereth in summer is a wise son: but he that sleepeth in harvest is a son that causeth shame.* **Proverbs 10:4-5,** *The thoughts of the diligent tend only to plenteousness; but of every one that is hasty only to want.* **Proverbs 21:5,** *He that tilleth his land shall be satisfied with bread: but he that followeth vain persons is void of understanding.* **Proverbs 12:11, 19** *He that tilleth his land shall have plenty of bread: but he that followeth after vain persons shall have poverty enough. 20 A faithful man shall*

abound with blessings: but he that maketh haste to be rich shall not be innocent. **Proverbs 28:19-20,** The slothful man roasteth not that which he took in hunting: but the substance of a diligent man is precious. **Proverbs 12:27,** Wealth gotten by vanity shall be diminished: but he that gathereth by labour shall increase. **Proverbs 13:11,** The sluggard will not plow by reason of the cold; therefore shall he beg in harvest, and have nothing. **Proverbs 20:4,** There is treasure to be desired and oil in the dwelling of the wise; but a foolish man spendeth it up. **Proverbs 21:20,** *1* A good name is rather to be chosen than great riches, and loving favour rather than silver and gold. *2* The rich and poor meet together: the LORD is the maker of them all. *3* A prudent man foreseeth the evil, and hideth himself: but the simple pass on, and are punished. *4* By humility and the fear of the LORD are riches, and honour, and life. **Proverbs 22:1-4,** The rich ruleth over the poor, and the borrower is servant to the lender. **Proverbs 22:7,** Wisdom is too high for a fool: he openeth not his mouth in the gate. **Proverbs 24:7,** *13* She seeketh wool, and flax, and worketh willingly with her hands. *14* She is like the merchants' ships; she bringeth her food from afar. **Proverbs 31:13-14,** She considereth a field, and buyeth it: with the fruit of her hands she planteth a vineyard. **Proverbs 31:16,** She is not afraid of the snow for her household: for all her household are clothed with scarlet. **Proverbs 31:21,** She maketh fine linen, and selleth it; and delivereth girdles unto the merchant. **Proverbs 31:24)**

2. Saving is the opposite of borrowing. It is work now to enjoy later.

3. Investments are not only wise financially and obedience to the Bible, but also the building blocks of the economy.

H. Estates, Wills, Inheritances

1. God requires us to provide for our own (**I Tim. 5:8,** *But if any provide not for his own, and specially for those of his own house, he hath denied the faith, and is worse than an infidel.* **1 Timothy 5:8**)
2. Children's marriages are to be affected to keep inheritances right (**Ezra 9:12:** *Now therefore give not your daughters unto their sons, neither take their daughters unto your sons, nor seek their peace or their wealth for ever: that ye may be strong, and eat the good of the land, and leave it for an inheritance to your children for ever.* **Ezra 9:12**)
3. The Bible teaches that sons should be given a house (**Prov.19:14:** *House and riches are the inheritance of fathers: and a prudent wife is from the LORD.* **Proverbs 19:14**), grandchildren an inheritance (**Prov. 13:22,** *A good man leaveth an inheritance to his children's children: and the wealth of the sinner is laid up for the just.* **Proverbs 13:22**), and those who love understanding substance (**Prov. 8:14-21: 14** *Counsel is mine, and sound wisdom: I am understanding; I have strength.* **15** *By me kings reign, and princes decree justice.* **16** *By me princes rule, and nobles, even all the judges of the earth.* **17** *I love them that love me; and those that seek me early shall find me.* **18** *Riches and honour are with me; yea, durable riches and righteousness.* **19** *My fruit is better than gold, yea, than fine gold; and my revenue than choice silver.* **20** *I lead in the way*

CHAPTER 10: FINANCIAL OPERATIONS

of righteousness, in the midst of the paths of judgment: **21** *That I may cause those that love me to inherit substance; and I will fill their treasures.* **Proverbs 8:14-21**)! The just can receive from the sinner (**Prov. 28:8:** *He that by usury and unjust gain increaseth his substance, he shall gather it for him that will pity the poor.* **Proverbs 28:8**).

4. Hurry or haste to get an inheritance may work, but will fail in the long run (**Prov. 20:21:** *An inheritance may be gotten hastily at the beginning; but the end thereof shall not be blessed.* **Proverbs 20:21**). Greed, covetousness, and family problems often show at inheritance time (**Luke 12:13-15: 15:11-32:** *13 And one of the company said unto him, Master, speak to my brother, that he divide the inheritance with me. 14 And he said unto him, Man, who made me a judge or a divider over you? 15 And he said unto them, Take heed, and beware of covetousness: for a man's life consisteth not in the abundance of the things which he possesseth.* **Luke 12:13-15, 11** *And he said, A certain man had two sons: 12 And the younger of them said to his father, Father, give me the portion of goods that falleth to me. And he divided unto them his living. 13 And not many days after the younger son gathered all together, and took his journey into a far country, and there wasted his substance with riotous living. 14 And when he had spent all, there arose a mighty famine in that land; and he began to be in want. 15 And he went and joined himself to a citizen of that country; and he sent him into his fields to feed swine. 16 And he would fain have filled his belly with the husks that the swine did eat: and no man gave unto him. 17 And when he came to himself, he said, How many hired servants of my father's have bread enough and to spare, and I perish with hunger! 18 I will arise and go to my*

father, and will say unto him, Father, I have sinned against heaven, and before thee, **19** *And am no more worthy to be called thy son: make me as one of thy hired servants.* **20** *And he arose, and came to his father. But when he was yet a great way off, his father saw him, and had compassion, and ran, and fell on his neck, and kissed him.* **21** *And the son said unto him, Father, I have sinned against heaven, and in thy sight, and am no more worthy to be called thy son.* **22** *But the father said to his servants, Bring forth the best robe, and put it on him; and put a ring on his hand, and shoes on his feet:* **23** *And bring hither the fatted calf, and kill it; and let us eat, and be merry:* **24** *For this my son was dead, and is alive again; he was lost, and is found. And they began to be merry.* **25** *Now his elder son was in the field: and as he came and drew nigh to the house, he heard musick and dancing.* **26** *And he called one of the servants, and asked what these things meant.* **27** *And he said unto him, Thy brother is come; and thy father hath killed the fatted calf, because he hath received him safe and sound.* **28** *And he was angry, and would not go in: therefore came his father out, and intreated him.* **29** *And he answering said to his father, Lo, these many years do I serve thee, neither transgressed I at any time thy commandment: and yet thou never gavest me a kid, that I might make merry with my friends:* **30** *But as soon as this thy son was come, which hath devoured thy living with harlots, thou hast killed for him the fatted calf.* **31** *And he said unto him, Son, thou art ever with me, and all that I have is thine.* **32** *It was meet that we should make merry, and be glad: for this thy brother was dead, and is alive again; and was lost, and is found.* **Luke 15:11-32**).

5. Don't count on others appreciating or properly using your estate (**Eccle. 2:18, 19:** *18 Yea, I hated all my labour which I had taken under the sun: because I should leave it unto the man that shall be after me. 19 And who knoweth whether he shall be a wise man or a fool? yet shall he have rule over all my labour wherein I have laboured, and wherein I have shewed myself wise under the sun. This is also vanity.* **Ecclesiastes 2:18-19**)
6. Don't forget to tithe on any income received from an inheritance.

I. Giving

1. Giving is not losing your money, but rather investing it. Do it wisely, bountifully, Biblically, and you will reap greatly.
2. John Wesley taught, "Earn all you can and save all you can, so that you can give all you can as long as you can."
3. Giving is how we transfer carnal wealth into spiritual capital and then deposit it in heaven. God then provides for us here.

J. Covetousness or Contentment

1. Covetousness is a sin of the heart and defiles us (**Mark 7:21-23; Luke 12:15, 34; Rom. 1:29, 32: 21** *For from within, out of the heart of men, proceed evil thoughts, adulteries, fornications, murders, 22 Thefts, covetousness, wickedness, deceit, lasciviousness, an evil eye, blasphemy, pride, foolishness: 23 All these evil things come from within, and defile the man.* **Mark 7:21-23,** *And he said unto them, Take heed, and*

beware of covetousness: for a man's life consisteth not in the abundance of the things which he possesseth. **Luke 12:15**). It is a proper cause for church discipline (**I Cor. 5:11; 6:9-11; Eph. 5:3-5,** *But now I have written unto you not to keep company, if any man that is called a brother be a fornicator, or covetous, or an idolater, or a railer, or a drunkard, or an extortioner; with such an one no not to eat.* **1 Corinthians 5:11, 9** *Know ye not that the unrighteous shall not inherit the kingdom of God? Be not deceived: neither fornicators, nor idolaters, nor adulterers, nor effeminate, nor abusers of themselves with mankind,* **10** *Nor thieves, nor covetous, nor drunkards, nor revilers, nor extortioners, shall inherit the kingdom of God.* **11** *And such were some of you: but ye are washed, but ye are sanctified, but ye are justified in the name of the Lord Jesus, and by the Spirit of our God.* **1 Corinthians 6:9-11, 3** *But fornication, and all uncleanness, or covetousness, let it not be once named among you, as becometh saints;* **4** *Neither filthiness, nor foolish talking, nor jesting, which are not convenient: but rather giving of thanks.* **5** *For this ye know, that no whoremonger, nor unclean person, nor covetous man, who is an idolater, hath any inheritance in the kingdom of Christ and of God.* **Ephesians 5:3-5**).

2. Covetousness is a form of idolatry (**Col. 3:5:** *Mortify therefore your members which are upon the earth; fornication, uncleanness, inordinate affection, evil concupiscence, and covetousness, which is idolatry:* **Colossians 3:5**), disqualification for the ministry (**I Tim. 3:3,** *Not given to wine, no striker, not greedy of filthy lucre; but patient, not a brawler, not covetous;* **1**

Timothy 3:3), and a mark of apostasy (**II Tim. 3:2; II Pet. 2:3, 14-16:** *For men shall be lovers of their own selves, covetous, boasters, proud, blasphemers, disobedient to parents, unthankful, unholy,* **2 Timothy 3:2,** *And through covetousness shall they with feigned words make merchandise of you: whose judgment now of a long time lingereth not, and their damnation slumbereth not.* **2 Peter 2:3, 14** *Having eyes full of adultery, and that cannot cease from sin; beguiling unstable souls: an heart they have exercised with covetous practices; cursed children:* **15** *Which have forsaken the right way, and are gone astray, following the way of Balaam the son of Bosor, who loved the wages of unrighteousness;* **16** *But was rebuked for his iniquity: the dumb ass speaking with man's voice forbad the madness of the prophet.* **2 Peter 2:14-16**). It is the root of **all** evil (**I Tim. 6:10**).

3. **Contentment is the opposite of covetousness** (**Heb. 13:5,** *Let your conversation be without covetousness; and be content with such things as ye have: for he hath said, I will never leave thee, nor forsake thee.* **Hebrews 13:5**); is not laziness, and a producer of peace. It involves being content with your wages (**Luke 3:14:** *And the soldiers likewise demanded of him, saying, And what shall we do? And he said unto them, Do violence to no man, neither accuse any falsely; and be content with your wages.* **Luke 3:14**), your state (**Phil. 4:1-13:** *1 Therefore, my brethren dearly beloved and longed for, my joy and crown, so stand fast in the Lord, my dearly beloved. 2 I beseech Euodias, and beseech Syntyche, that they be of*

the same mind in the Lord. 3 And I intreat thee also, true yokefellow, help those women which laboured with me in the gospel, with Clement also, and with other my fellowlabourers, whose names are in the book of life. 4 Rejoice in the Lord alway: and again I say, Rejoice. 5 Let your moderation be known unto all men. The Lord is at hand. 6 Be careful for nothing; but in every thing by prayer and supplication with thanksgiving let your requests be made known unto God. 7 And the peace of God, which passeth all understanding, shall keep your hearts and minds through Christ Jesus. 8 Finally, brethren, whatsoever things are true, whatsoever things are honest, whatsoever things are just, whatsoever things are pure, whatsoever things are lovely, whatsoever things are of good report; if there be any virtue, and if there be any praise, think on these things. 9 Those things, which ye have both learned, and received, and heard, and seen in me, do: and the God of peace shall be with you. 10 But I rejoiced in the Lord greatly, that now at the last your care of me hath flourished again; wherein ye were also careful, but ye lacked opportunity. 11 Not that I speak in respect of want: for I have learned, in whatsoever state I am, therewith to be content. 12 I know both how to be abased, and I know how to abound: every where and in all things I am instructed both to be full and to be hungry, both to abound and to suffer need. 13 I can do all things through Christ which strengtheneth me. **Philippians 4:1-13**), food and raiment (**I Tim 6:6-8: 6** *But godliness with contentment is great gain. 7 For we brought nothing into this world, and it is certain we can carry nothing* *out. 8 And having food and raiment let us be therewith content.* **1 Timothy 6:6-8**), and such things as you have (**Heb. 13:5:** *Let your conversation be without covetousness; and be content with such things as ye have: for he hath said, I will never leave thee, nor forsake thee.* **Hebrews 13:5**).

CHAPTER XI

RECREATIONAL POSSIBILITIES

A. **Family Time**
1. Opportunity to bond the family together during mutual activities.
2. Joint exercise, activity, competition, and learning prove helpful to the individuals as well as the family unit. Attitudes and relationships within the family often surface to where they can be dealt with.

B. **Vacations**
1. These are taught by Jesus (**Mark:6:30-32:** *30 And the apostles gathered themselves together unto Jesus, and told him all things, both what they had done, and what they had taught. 31 And he said unto them, Come ye yourselves apart into a desert place, and rest a while: for there were many coming and going, and they had no leisure so much as to eat. 32 And they departed into a desert place by ship privately.* **Mark 6:30-32**)
2. They should provide rest, refreshing, and recharging for future labor.
3. Often they can be educational and provide an appreciation for God, country and local church.

C. **Sports**
1. There are plenty of references and examples in both O.T and N.T.
2. While these may become an idol, and all too often do, there is a proper place for them in the Christian family.

3. Benefits include physical well-being, development of teamwork, concepts, progress in control of emotions, practice in stress-handling, learning to strive for success, and growth of competitive abilities.

D. Bible Conferences, Camping, Camp Meetings

1. The. O.T. taught time for seven feasts at three times a year.
2. The gathering of God's people by families in one place from scattered locations is God-ordained. It not only makes for healthier families and progress spiritually, but also opens up better understanding of others and special opportunities for young people to meet others of their age and beliefs.

E. Considerations

1. The family benefits from such.
2. Opportunities for contacts and Gospel witness are plentiful.
3. Biblically it is usually best to keep it simple, natural, and inexpensive. Creativeness flourishes best under these circumstances.

CHAPTER XII

RESTRAINING ADULT CHILDREN FROM SIN

A. Responsibility

I Sam. 3:13

For I have told him that I will judge his house for ever for the iniquity which he knoweth; because his sons made themselves vile, and he restrained them not. **1 Samuel 3:13**

> 1) Eli was responsible to restrain his sons from sin: "Restrain" means putting the brakes on, slowing down, holding back.
> "Restrain" does not necessarily mean stopping or correcting.

I Sam. 2:12-17, 22

***12** Now the sons of Eli were sons of Belial; they knew not the LORD. **13** And the priests' custom with the people was, that, when any man offered sacrifice, the priest's servant came, while the flesh was in seething, with a fleshhook of three teeth in his hand; **14** And he struck it into the pan, or kettle, or caldron, or pot; all that the fleshhook brought up the priest took for himself. So they did in Shiloh unto all the Israelites that came thither. **15** Also before they burnt the fat, the priest's servant came, and said to the man that sacrificed, Give flesh to roast for the priest; for he will not have sodden flesh of thee, but raw. **16** And if any man said unto him, Let them not fail to burn the fat presently, and then take as much as thy soul desireth; then he would answer him, Nay; but thou shalt give it me now: and if not, I will take it by force. **17** Wherefore the sin of the young men was very great before*

CHAPTER 12: RESTRAINING ADULT CHILDREN FROM SIN

the LORD: for men abhorred the offering of the LORD. **1 Samuel 2:12-17,** *Now Eli was very old, and heard all that his sons did unto all Israel; and how they lay with the women that assembled at the door of the tabernacle of the congregation.* **1 Samuel 2:22**

    2) Eli's sons were not small children, but adults:

2:12-17	Took food for a home
	Capable of taking from adults by force
2:22	Sin of adultery
3:13	Train a child (**Prov. 22:6:** *Train up a child in the way he should go: and when he is old, he will not depart from it.* **Proverbs 22:6**) and restrain an adult

I Sam. 2:25; 3:13, 14

If one man sin against another, the judge shall judge him: but if a man sin against the LORD, who shall intreat for him? Notwithstanding they hearkened not unto the voice of their father, because the LORD would slay them. **1 Samuel 2:25, 13** *For I have told him that I will judge his house for ever for the iniquity which he knoweth; because his sons made themselves vile, and he restrained them not.* **14** *And therefore I have sworn unto the house of Eli, that the iniquity of Eli's house shall not be purged with sacrifice nor offering for ever.* **1 Samuel 3:13-14**

    3) Realize that there is a point beyond which there is no recovery:

    "Restraint" must occur **before** this point is reached. Too late will never succeed (**2:25**).

I Sam. 3:13 (see verse above)

    4) "Restrain" is the opposite of:
        a) ignoring the issue

b) defending the son or daughter
c) supporting them in their evil choices of sin
d) mildly approaching the issue without progress (**2:23-25a:** *23 And he said unto them, Why do ye such things? for I hear of your evil dealings by all this people. 24 Nay, my sons; for it is no good report that I hear: ye make the LORD'S people to transgress. 25 If one man sin against another, the judge shall judge him: but if a man sin against the LORD, who shall intreat for him? Notwithstanding they hearkened not unto the voice of their father, because the LORD would slay them.* **1 Samuel 2:23-25**).

5) If God held Eli responsible in the O.T., how much more are we responsible today? If Eli could have restrained his adult sons, how much more can we today?
   a) Have more power under Grace than under Law
   b) Have more promises, light, teaching, Bible, and experience of years than Eli had
   c) (**Luke 12:48: Jude 4; Heb 11:39, 40; II Cor. 1:20:** *But he that knew not, and did commit things worthy of stripes, shall be beaten with few stripes. For unto whomsoever much is given, of him shall be much required: and to whom men have committed much, of him they will ask the more.* **Luke 12:48,** *For there are certain men crept in unawares, who were before of old ordained to this condemnation,*

ungodly men, turning the grace of our God into lasciviousness, and denying the only Lord God, and our Lord Jesus Christ. **Jude 1:4, 39** And these all, having obtained a good report through faith, received not the promise: **40** God having provided some better thing for us, that they without us should not be made perfect. **Hebrews 11:39-40,** For all the promises of God in him are yea, and in him Amen, unto the glory of God by us. **2 Corinthians 1:20**)

6) Some excuses used to avoid responsibility for restraint:
   a) Fatalism – "it's the will of God"
   b) False spirituality "I turned them over to God"
   c) Quitting "I have done all that I can"

B. Opportunity
I Sam. 3:13 (see verse above)

1) Since Eli was responsible to restrain his adult sons, we must be able to restrain our adult children
   We are not helpless before our children's enemies:
   a) world (**I John 5:4, 5: 4** For whatsoever is born of God overcometh the world: and this is the victory that overcometh the world, even our faith. **5** Who is he that overcometh the world, but he that believeth that Jesus is the Son of God? **1 John 5:4-5**)

b) flesh (**Rom. 8:9-13; Gal. 5:16-18:** *9 But ye are not in the flesh, but in the Spirit, if so be that the Spirit of God dwell in you. Now if any man have not the Spirit of Christ, he is none of his. 10 And if Christ be in you, the body is dead because of sin; but the Spirit is life because of righteousness. 11 But if the Spirit of him that raised up Jesus from the dead dwell in you, he that raised up Christ from the dead shall also quicken your mortal bodies by his Spirit that dwelleth in you. 12 Therefore, brethren, we are debtors, not to the flesh, to live after the flesh. 13 For if ye live after the flesh, ye shall die: but if ye through the Spirit do mortify the deeds of the body, ye shall live.* **Romans 8:9-13, 16,** *This I say then, Walk in the Spirit, and ye shall not fulfil the lust of the flesh. 17 For the flesh lusteth against the Spirit, and the Spirit against the flesh: and these are contrary the one to the other: so that ye cannot do the things that ye would. 18 But if ye be led of the Spirit, ye are not under the law.* **Galatians 5:16-18**)

c) devil (**Rev. 12:10, 11:** *10 And I heard a loud voice saying in heaven, Now is come salvation, and strength, and the kingdom of our God, and the power of his Christ: for the accuser of our brethren is cast down, which accused them before our God day and night. 11 And they overcame him by the blood of the Lamb, and by the word of their testimony; and they loved not their lives unto the death.* **Revelation 12:10-11**)

CHAPTER 12: RESTRAINING ADULT CHILDREN FROM SIN

    2) *We are given many tools.*
        a) various tools for various needs
        b) If milder tools won't work, then stronger tools must be used (**I Sam. 2:23-25a**: see the verse above)

C. Methods or Tools
Prov. 22:6

Train up a child in the way he should go: and when he is old, he will not depart from it. **Proverbs 22:6**

    1) The amount of foundation in training as young children will give you a basis to appeal to in talking and praying.

Acts 3:12

And when Peter saw it, he answered unto the people, Ye men of Israel, why marvel ye at this? or why look ye so earnestly on us, as though by our own power or holiness we had made this man to walk? **Acts 3:12**

    2) The holy life of the parent(s) often impacts the child. The holier the greater the impact (**II Tim. 1:5; Matt.5:12, 13:** *When I call to remembrance the unfeigned faith that is in thee, which dwelt first in thy grandmother Lois, and thy mother Eunice; and I am persuaded that in thee also.* **2 Timothy 1:5, 12,** *Rejoice, and be exceeding glad: for great is your reward in heaven: for so persecuted they the prophets which were before you.* **13** *Ye are the salt of the earth: but if the salt have lost his savour, wherewith shall it be salted? it is thenceforth good for nothing, but to*

be cast out, and to be trodden under foot of men. **Matthew 5:12-13**)

Matt: 7:7, 8

7 Ask, and it shall be given you; seek, and ye shall find; knock, and it shall be opened unto you: 8 For every one that asketh receiveth; and he that seeketh findeth; and to him that knocketh it shall be opened. **Matthew 7:7-8**

> 3) Prayer brings many answers. The various laws, promises, principles, levels, and examples of prayer reveal what can be done (**James 4:2; 5:16:** *Ye lust, and have not: ye kill, and desire to have, and cannot obtain: ye fight and war, yet ye have not, because ye ask not.* **James 4:2,** *Confess your faults one to another, and pray one for another, that ye may be healed. The effectual fervent prayer of a righteous man availeth much.* **James 5:16** etc).

Gen. 26:34, 35; 28: 6-9

34 And Esau was forty years old when he took to wife Judith the daughter of Beeri the Hittite, and Bashemath the daughter of Elon the Hittite: 35 Which were a grief of mind unto Isaac and to Rebekah. **Genesis 26:34-35, 6** *When Esau saw that Isaac had blessed Jacob, and sent him away to Padanaram, to take him a wife from thence; and that as he blessed him he gave him a charge, saying, Thou shalt not take a wife of the daughters of Canaan; 7 And that Jacob obeyed his father and his mother, and was gone to Padanaram; 8 And Esau seeing that the daughters of Canaan pleased not Isaac his father; 9 Then went Esau unto Ishmael, and took unto the wives which he had Mahalath the daughter of Ishmael Abraham's son, the sister of Nebajoth, to be his wife.* **Genesis 28:6-9**

CHAPTER 12: RESTRAINING ADULT CHILDREN FROM SIN

    4) Withholding approval of their life, their actions, and/or their choices will impact them.
    5) **Gen. 49:5-7:** *5 Simeon and Levi are brethren; instruments of cruelty are in their habitations. 6 O my soul, come not thou into their secret; unto their assembly, mine honour, be not thou united: for in their anger they slew a man, and in their selfwill they digged down a wall. 7 Cursed be their anger, for it was fierce; and their wrath, for it was cruel: I will divide them in Jacob, and scatter them in Israel.* **Genesis 49:5-7**
    6) Public denouncement and/or exposure is a strong tool to be used with caution. *For example:*
        a) Aaron could not even attend his two sons' funeral (Nadab and Abihu) because of their sin (**Lev. 10**).
        b) Noah cursed his grandson, Canaan (**Gen. 9:25, 26:** *25 And he said, Cursed be Canaan; a servant of servants shall he be unto his brethren. 26 And he said, Blessed be the LORD God of Shem; and Canaan shall be his servant.* **Genesis 9:25-26**).

I Sam. 3:12-14

    7) Family issues are affected by sin.
        a) Eli's family lost the High Priesthood.
        b) Samuel's family lost the rulership (**I Sam.**).
        c) David's family suffered as well as David (**II Sam.**).

Family honor, family name, family blessing, family future and more are hurt when sin brings family disgrace.

James 1:6-8

6 But let him ask in faith, nothing wavering. For he that wavereth is like a wave of the sea driven with the wind and tossed. 7 For let not that man think that he shall receive any thing of the Lord. 8 A double minded man is unstable in all his ways. **James 1:6-8**

> 8) Unwavering convictions are needed. We can't have two sets of convictions – one for others and softer ones for our own families.

II Tim. 2:24-26

24 And the servant of the Lord must not strive; but be gentle unto all men, apt to teach, patient, 25 In meekness instructing those that oppose themselves; if God peradventure will give them repentance to the acknowledging of the truth; 26 And that they may recover themselves out of the snare of the devil, who are taken captive by him at his will. **2 Timothy 2:24-26**

> 9) Gentleness and meekness without compromise are needed. Threats, shouting, force, or brutality will not be used by God (**Jude 10, 13; II Pet. 2:12:** *But these speak evil of those things which they know not: but what they know naturally, as brute beasts, in those things they corrupt themselves.* **Jude 1:10,** *Raging waves of the sea, foaming out their own shame; wandering stars, to whom is reserved the blackness of darkness for ever.* **Jude 1:13,** *But these, as natural brute beasts, made to be taken and destroyed, speak evil of the things that they understand not; and shall utterly perish in their own corruption;* **2 Peter 2:12**)

CHAPTER 12: RESTRAINING ADULT CHILDREN FROM SIN

Luke 15:11-32

11 And he said, A certain man had two sons: 12 And the younger of them said to his father, Father, give me the portion of goods that falleth to me. And he divided unto them his living. 13 And not many days after the younger son gathered all together, and took his journey into a far country, and there wasted his substance with riotous living. 14 And when he had spent all, there arose a mighty famine in that land; and he began to be in want. 15 And he went and joined himself to a citizen of that country; and he sent him into his fields to feed swine. 16 And he would fain have filled his belly with the husks that the swine did eat: and no man gave unto him. 17 And when he came to himself, he said, How many hired servants of my father's have bread enough and to spare, and I perish with hunger! 18 I will arise and go to my father, and will say unto him, Father, I have sinned against heaven, and before thee, 19 And am no more worthy to be called thy son: make me as one of thy hired servants. 20 And he arose, and came to his father. But when he was yet a great way off, his father saw him, and had compassion, and ran, and fell on his neck, and kissed him. 21 And the son said unto him, Father, I have sinned against heaven, and in thy sight, and am no more worthy to be called thy son. 22 But the father said to his servants, Bring forth the best robe, and put it on him; and put a ring on his hand, and shoes on his feet: 23 And bring hither the fatted calf, and kill it; and let us eat, and be merry: 24 For this my son was dead, and is alive again; he was lost, and is found. And they began to be merry. 25 Now his elder son was in the field: and as he came and drew nigh to the house, he heard musick and dancing. 26 And he called one of the servants, and asked what these things meant. 27 And he said unto him, Thy brother is come; and thy father hath killed the fatted calf, because he hath received him safe and sound. 28 And he was angry, and would not go in: therefore came his father out, and intreated him. 29 And he answering said to his father, Lo, these many years do I serve thee, neither transgressed I at any time thy commandment: and yet thou *never gavest me a kid, that I might make merry with my friends: **30** But as soon as this thy son was come, which hath devoured thy living with harlots, thou hast killed for him the fatted calf. **31** And he said unto him, Son, thou art ever with me, and all that I have is thine. **32** It was meet that we should make merry, and be glad: for this thy brother was dead, and is alive again; and was lost, and is found.* **Luke 15:11-32**

> 10) Sin must not be sanctioned. The son returned to the father in repentance. There was no bartering or negotiation over sin.

Gal. 5:7, 8

***7** Ye did run well; who did hinder you that ye should not obey the truth? **8** This persuasion cometh not of him that calleth you.* **Galatians 5:7-8**

> 11) Warning the child of sowing and reaping often restrains them.

I Sam. 2:23-25

***23** And he said unto them, Why do ye such things? for I hear of your evil dealings by all this people. **24** Nay, my sons; for it is no good report that I hear: ye make the LORD'S people to transgress. **25** If one man sin against another, the judge shall judge him: but if a man sin against the LORD, who shall intreat for him? Notwithstanding they hearkened not unto the voice of their father, because the LORD would slay them.* **1 Samuel 2:23-25**

> 12) Reasoning with them may help them think of the seriousness of their sin. Remember how God reasons with us (**Isa. 1:18:** *Come now, and let us reason together, saith the LORD: though your sins be as scarlet, they shall be as white as snow; though they be red like crimson, they shall be as wool.* **Isaiah 1:18**).

CHAPTER 12: RESTRAINING ADULT CHILDREN FROM SIN

II Tim. 2:24-26

24 And the servant of the Lord must not strive; but be gentle unto all men, apt to teach, patient, 25 In meekness instructing those that oppose themselves; if God peradventure will give them repentance to the acknowledging of the truth; 26 And that they may recover themselves out of the snare of the devil, who are taken captive by him at his will. **2 Timothy 2:24-26**

> 13) Scriptural knowledge is needed
>   a) to be able to teach
>   b) to understand what is happening
>   c) to know who we are in Christ
>   d) to know tools of priest of family and head of home
> 14) Pleading with genuine tears of a broken heart may help turn the tide.

Heb. 11:24-26

24 By faith Moses, when he was come to years, refused to be called the son of Pharaoh's daughter; 25 Choosing rather to suffer affliction with the people of God, than to enjoy the pleasures of sin for a season; 26 Esteeming the reproach of Christ greater riches than the treasures in Egypt: for he had respect unto the recompence of the reward. **Hebrews 11:24-26**

> 15) Discussion of their desired long-range future may help them see that sin pleases only for a short time. Talk of personal vision, family vision, and loss of direction, goals, closed doors, self-set limits, and actual accomplishments.

ABOUT THE AUTHOR

J. PAUL RENO has been a pastor in Ohio and Maryland since 1968. During this time he has also been involved in church planting, training men for the ministry and speaking on mission fields in Europe, the Middle East, Africa, South America and Mexico. The church he presently pastors has just passed sending 3 and 2/3 million dollars to missions. He continues to speak at various Bible conferences, camp meetings and local churches. He presently serves on the Board of Directors for the Conversion Center, which is headquartered in Hagerstown, Maryland. Pastor Reno recently was honored with the prestigious award, "Defender of the Scriptures," by the King James Bible Research Council.

He is also the author of *To Fight or Not to Fight*, *Daniel Nash: Prevailing Prince of Prayer*, *Investing for Eternity*, *Studies in Bible Doctrine* as well as over fifty pamphlets and booklets on salvation, the Christian life, Bible doctrine and the King James Version. His wife, Carolyn authored *Almost But Lost*, available as a free ebook download at:
http://www.theoldpathspublications.com/Pages/Free.htm.

www.ingramcontent.com/pod-product-compliance
Lightning Source LLC
LaVergne TN
LVHW051134080426
835510LV00018B/2401